MARRIAGE IN THE *FAST* LANE

A One-Month Survival Manual For Christian Marriages In Contemporary Society

By
Perry C. Cotham

MARRIAGE IN THE *FAST* LANE

*A One-Month Survival Manual
For Christian Marriages
In Contemporary Society*

By
Perry C. Cotham

20th Century Christian Foundation
2809 Granny White Pike
Nashville, TN 37204

Contents

Preface

Why Another Book On Marriage?

In the past few years it has become all too fashionable to say that the American family is in trouble. Since the late 60s the notion that American family life is in danger, even in a state of crisis, has been a prominent theme in our mass media. There is a great deal of concern about the survival of the nuclear family, the traditional family structure where the father pursues his vocation or profession and the mother works at home and provides emotional support and child guidance. Concerned Christians and activist groups, such as Moral Majority, can point to statistics showing an increase in divorce rates, a slight decline in marriage rates, and a dramatic decline in birth rates. The main fact about family life today is that traditionally sanctified beliefs and practices have come to be openly challenged.

As we all know, family life and sex roles have emerged as con troversial public issues. It is not simply coincidental that most of the crucial social issues confronting our society in the 80s are also issues which are of central importance to the American family system as a basic social institution. The family and the society-at-large face common issues because the threads of family life in our culture have been so thoroughly interwoven with the general fabric of the society as to be almost of one cloth Social issues such as the necessity of marriage itself; the desirability of having children; definitions of masculinity and feminity; the rights and obligations of children and parents to each other; questions concerning legal reforms in the areas of divorce and abortion; and finally, even questions concerning the need or desirability of marital fidelity—all of these are family issues and all the traditional doctrine is now open to question and debate.

When the general society looks to the church for some answers, it may not be heartened by what it sees or hears. Marriage failure is certainly not limited to those couples who make no profession at being Christian, an understatement for certain. What congregation has not been deeply affected by marital trouble among its own ranks? Is there a congregation which has not been stunned by the sudden revelation of a grave marital problem within what appeared to be one of its staunchest, most faithful families? Is there any marriage—be it the marriage of the preacher, an elder, a church school executive, a Christian educator, a renowned evangelist—that is exempt from the possibility of serious marital difficulty? We all know the answers to such questions. Sometimes the bigger, stronger, and more influential church leaders appear, the harder they fall when marital impasse is revealed. This is the very route through which many of us are learning humility.

The sad fact is that this generation is raising a generation of children who observe their parents' failures and then develop a fear of marriage. Young adolescents have suffered through the divorce of their parents and have vowed that they would never marry. They will marry, most likely, but perhaps not until after experimentation with various alternative lifestyles. A good word for married life is difficult to hear in many quarters; and, at the present time, youth seem to speak less about dating and courtship and more in terms of involvement. In light of all we've said thus far, the church has an awesome responsibility to address these issues and to offer counsel and support for all kinds of families which still seek to be Christian families.

This is a book about Christian marriage. It is written by a Christian for Christians who are married already. The chief concern here is the marriage relationship; other family issues, such as parenting, will not be discussed except incidentally. Is Christian marriage more difficult to sustain than marriages entered by those who profess no Christian faith? Well, such a question is not easily answered. On the one hand, Christian marriages have specific support and foundational undergirding which is unavailable in non-Christian unions. On the other hand, there are some problems peculiar to Christian marriage that surface out of the issues of authority relationships, male-female roles, and the Biblical doctrine on divorce and remarriage; and Christians seem to invite problems by approaching some Biblical values (*eg.,* fidelity) in a mechanical and legalistic way. This book will reflect the uniqueness of Christian marriage and in the first chapter our major assumptions are stated.

Why another book on marriage? There are numerous books currently available—many of them saying the same thing. The big problem is that too many of them are never read and the advice that is read is often neglected. One of our goals is to present some material compellingly and interestingly. This book is written in an informal style and we have not shunned a little humor and wit. But, most important, our goal has been to address some old problems with some new insight. Society is not static and change is constant, so the pressures and challenges to Christian marriage will contine to be altered. Therefore, there will always be a need for a realistic and relevant application of Biblical principles to contemporary situations.

You may be interested chiefly in doctrinal exposition, with a focus on the critical passages of Scripture that deal with divorce and remarriage. If so, you will be disappointed. A number of books address such doctrinal issues—this book is not one of them. The aim here is to be practical. Every marriage relationship has many untapped potentialities. As Christians we have explicit instruction: "Let us speak the truth in love; so shall we fully grow up into Christ. He is the head, and on him the whole body depends. Bonded and knit together by every constituent joint, the whole frame grows through the due activity of each part, and builds itself up in love" (Eph. 4:15,16 NEB). Is there a better place to follow this admonition than in our marriages?

Perhaps the ultimate and most obvious test of a successful marriage is whether the two partners remain married for a lifetime or terminate the marriage by divorce. But the Apostle Paul, though not speaking specifically about marriage in the above passage, suggests that Christians be concerned with other measures—whether the marriage enables the truth to be communicated in love and whether the marriage enables each partner to develop to a high level of emotional maturity, happiness, and personal fulfillment.

This book does not provide a direct path to a happy and fulfilling marriage. Nobody can do that, nor can a book. This volume will supply a little information, raise some important questions and, most importantly, direct your practical efforts toward enrichment of your marriage. It will not matter how briefly or how long you have been married; at any point in your marriage you are either moving at some place in the direction of fulfillment or moving toward stagnation. We will not shrink from controversial issues and criticism nor deny personal biases; a volume lacking in such qualities will prove not only dull but misleading.

The Book Plan

A personal word here. A book this size could be read in two or three sittings. Which, if you are like me, will entice you to read through it rapidly. The topics are numerous and varied and the chapters are short. Entire volumes could be written on some of the chapter topics. My purpose is not exhaustive depth, but to provide some insights and direction I hope will be stimulating and helpful.

There are thirty chapters, one for each day of the month. Why not read a chapter a day with your mate in order to keep the priority of marriage enrichment in the forefront of your thinking continually!

It's not enough to write down some principles, instructions, and suggestions and then say to you "good luck." The Christian sees his/her marriage as a divinely ordained enterprise and an adventure in faith. Our vows are uttered before God and his divine direction and providential enabling are needed all along the years. To keep this idea before us, I have concluded each chapter with a prayer or meditational thought.

Acknowledgements

A lot of the ideas in this book are based on previously prepared class lectures and sermons and on experiences in pastoral counseling at the Westwood and Otter Creek congregations. In my own reading and preparation the published works of the following writers have proven to be the most useful: David Augsburger, Howard Clinebell, James Dobson, David Mace, Charles Shedd, Dwight H. Small, Lewis Smedes, and Paul Tournier. Scriptural references in this book, unless otherwise noted, are taken from the New International Version.

And finally, I would be remiss if I did not gratefully acknowledge the assistance of Emma Phillips, Otter Creek church secretary, who typed this manuscript for publication.

Perry C. Cotham
December, 1983

Chapter One

Can This Book Help Our Marriage?

Here we state ten assumptions about marital enrichment and if you can buy them your mental set should be right to profit from the pages to follow.

Our modern age is a time when marriage failure is frequent in the United States but also a time when there can be greater happiness and emotional fulfillment than in the past when there were fewer growth opportunities and man-woman relationships were more rigidly structured. In counseling we are dealing with theories and probabilities about personalities and relationships. Statistics can be marshalled, but underlying all that we will be saying are some important assumptions. In order for you to know where we are coming from, we state simply these assumptions. There are other assumptions, of course, but these ten are among the most significant ones. See if you agree with all of them.

I. There is no such thing as a perfect marriage. In fact, nothing in this life involving people is perfect—no social relationship, no vocational or professional relationship, no civic organization, no congregation. So why should we expect marriage to be perfect? Problems in marriage should not surprise us when we consider that marriage is the most difficult to maintain of all our social institutions, requiring maturity and flexibility on the part of both partners.

Family life has always been problematic in an emotional sense. Family life is the place where, as one person put it, "you're dealing with life-and-death voltages." The marriage experience is capable of evoking the worst in our character as well as the very best in our character. Dramatists and novelists, from the great Greek tragedians to the scriptwriters of hackneyed soap operas, have always portrayed the intimacies of family life in terms of love *and* hate, devotion *and* dereliction, sacrifice *and* spite, affection *and* cruelty. To the extent that both heaven and hell are experienced on earth, for most of us they are experienced in our marriages.

There is a corollary here: no two marriages are exactly alike. Every human is different from all others and when we bind two humans in a life-long commitment we witness the emergence of a unique and non-repeatable dynamism and phenonmenon. Fortunately, marriages have enough similarities that we are able to make generalizations and predictions about them. As helpful as general counsel may be, it must not be a substitute for face-to-face personal and marital counseling with a qualified therapist.

II. Where there is mutual commitment to the survival of the marriage, a troubled marriage can be saved. And a good marriage can be enriched where there is a mutual commitment to growth. We emphasize mutuality here. Frequently, marriage counselors and ministers will be summoned to aid in a situation where one partner is committed to continuing the marriage and the other is not. And one fact that many counselors learn early is that not everyone who says he/she is committed to continuing a marriage is, in reality, actually so committed.

III. Marriage by itself will not change one's basic personality structure. Radical Freudian psychologists hypothesize that a person's personality is determined before he completes the adolescent years. We do not accept such an extreme, pessimistic view; however, there is no doubt that a great part of our personality is developed before marriage and will remain constant. Undesirable traits are usually suppressed or minimized during courtship, only to surface after the wedding day. Marriage enrichment usually involves personality enrichment as well as relationship enrichment.

IV. Marriage begins with commitment, is rooted and nourished in love, is sustained by self-discipline, and is evaluated through growth experiences. We entered marriage at a wedding but we are continually moving *toward* marriage, toward a real unity that the legal document was intended to sustain. So we were married at one particular time in our family history, but we are continually moving toward ideal marriage.

V. We cannot change our partners directly, but we can change ourselves. We do not marry to reform another person. Can you honestly say to yourself, "I am the ony person responsible for my thinking and behavior. No one else is responsible for me but me!"

VI. Our partners' behavior does not cause our behavior. No one else can be made accountable or responsible for our own emotions and behavior. Seeking to place blame for marital difficulty and failure is usually self-defeating anyway. As an adult no one makes you do anything or feel any certain way. Your goal is to control yourself and analyze your options. When facing a vexing problem, do not say, "There's nothing I can do." We must behave as adults and in all situations treat our mates as adults.

VII. Marital difficulties are often rooted in patterns of mutually-defeating behavior. If one mate dares to change his behavior, the relationship can be improved. Waiting for the partner to change before we change is usually equivalent to no change. Love means that we dare to take a risk for the good of the marriage.

VIII. The lifeblood of a meaningful interpersonal relationship is effective communication. Marriages can survive without a lot of blessings, but not without good communication, which aims toward understanding and empathy.

IX. Pain and apprehension are a part of change and growth in relationships. Change disrupts the status quo with its comfortable patterns and introduces uncertainty. Personal and marital counseling which is effective can be very painful; little wonder that many discontinue counseling, sparing themselves the pain of self-knowledge and growth.

X. There is a spiritual dimension to the most fulfilling marriages. Christian marriage is unique, is truly creative and mutually enriching, and is inherently fortified against the evils and failures that lead to divorce. Christian marriage is not a lofty and unattainable ideal; it is a dynamic and noble enterprise in which we have the promise of the Lord's direction and power. The Bible is not, of course, a marriage counselor's handbook, but it is an authoritative resource book of divine principles and instructive narratives. For Christians, counsel for maintaining interpersonal relations must be rooted in the Bible's ethical doctrine. While emotional immaturity lies at the heart of much marital difficulty, to a large degree emotional immaturity may be linked to spiritual immaturity. We cannot hope to resolve our marital impasses unless we have first nurtured and mended our spiritual experience.

Scripture And Prayer

"Unless the Lord builds the house, its builders will have toiled in vain. Unless the Lord keeps watch over a city, in vain the watchman stands on guard" (Psalm 127:1). Lord, we want your direction and guardianship as we continue to build this home. Show us through your Word what you had in mind when you ordained marriage and how you want us now. Through Jesus. Amen.

What Were You Really Getting Into?

Here's a look at some categories of marriage that have developed over the course of social history as well as a brief statement of the strengths and weaknesses of each view of marriage.

Just as no two individuals are alike, no two relationships are exactly the same. Basic to close relationships is the existence of bonds, values, bargaining, and (with perhaps some rare exceptions) conflict. Marriage is as old as human history. And every marriage today is rooted in religious, cultural, ethnic, racial, and family pasts. Everything that we expect of marriage today has its roots in history. It would be fascinating to survey the history of marriage over the centuries, but we will not take the time for this now. Instead, let's look at some categories of marriage for nearly any age in history and as you read you might consider which perspective best describes your own marraige. Here we will use four general categories, though we must keep in mind that for most of us these simple categories are not separate and distinct.

Marriage For Convenience

Historically, most marriages were contracted for convenience. Such marriages provided practical solutions to specific problems. In rural America as late as the recent past, for example, the rugged life of the independent farmer made it imperative for him to have as much help as possible in working the crops, caring for the livestock, gathering the harvest, and going to market. A sturdy wife and energetic children were not simply a convenience but a necessity. In colonial and early American days, the family was the cornerstone of society; as in many agrarian societies today, it was next to impossible to survive outside the family. Everyone was expected to be married once he or she reached adulthood. During this early period single men and women were actively discouraged, at times even prohibited, from living alone or in pairs. Single women were ridiculed as "spinsters," "old maids," or "ancient virgins," and they generally lived with their families, which acted as the overseers of their virtue. Since marriage had profound economic and social consequences, parents often chose their children's mates, a custom still practiced throughout much of the world.

Marriage for *economic convenience* happens in many other ways. For example, two older people might decide that there are economic advantages for their living together rather than alone. Two persons who are wealthy may choose to meld their fortunes. One person may have considerable wealth or property holdings and the other wants and seeks it by the marriage route. A person may marry to protect a family fortune from exploitation. Of course, it is not necessary for a person or the other partner to be wealthy for a marriage of economic convenience to be arranged. One may seek a partner because he/she fits the image of what a spouse "should" be. A man or woman with a steady paycheck, even a modest one, often has great appeal. And quite often economic convenience will keep a marriage together even when neither partner is happy.

Marriage for *social convenience* or social conformity is fairly common. Young people may grow up hearing "Surely you want to get married! Who wants to be an oddball?" or "You don't want to wind up living all of life alone like your poor Aunt Laurel or your Uncle Harry!" Having been associated with Christian colleges, both as student and faculty member, I have heard numerous appeals to chapel audiences of college students for them not to neglect courtship and marriage opportunities. Apparently, it would have been a greater abdication of responsibility to leave college without a mate, or at least an engagement, than to leave without a diploma. I recall from undergraduate days the special anxieties of upperclassmen still in the ranks of unmarried, uncommitted, unattached and, even sadder, the unlikely-to-be-engaged as being the "junior jitters" and the "senior shakes." Many people find it more convenient and more comfortable simply to comply with what is expected of them than to adopt an alternate lifestyle. So they get married.

Akin to this is marriage for *psychological convenience*. People may want to be taken care of, to be placed on a pedestal, or to take care of another person. Psychological convenience is arranged when those marrying feel that they cannot bear to live alone. A young man or young woman may rush into a marriage in order to escape what he/she feels to be an unbearable homelife situation. Another may marry because all of his/her close friends have married and there is a felt need to do likewise. In the rush not to be left out of the married lifestyle, a person may see the available dating partner as a better mate than he/she actually is. In all of these cases some basic anxieties or fears interplay with the motivations for marriage; if these anxieties are not confronted realistically, such marriages may disintegrate.

Family convenience is related to psychological convenience in some cases. If a woman becomes pregnant outside of marriage, she and the father may get married in order to avoid a social stigma or to "give the baby a name," so that it will not be considered illegitimate. Approximately twenty percent of first-born children in the United States are conceived prior to marriage; obviously marriage for family convenience is fairly common.

There has long been marriage for *sexual convenience.* Many youth of recent times heard such loud and clear messages on the evils of premarital sex that marriage must have seemed little more than a haven of legalized sex. Despite changing sexual mores, strong religious and family sanctions against premarital sex are still operative among youth who find sex drives "almost impossible to control." Rather than succumb to sexual pressures and frustrations, they give into the social conformist ones.

Marriages for *political convenience* are not that common, but historically, there have been royal marriages which joined together clans, lands, fortune, and military strength. Undoubtedly, many of the marriages of Solomon were contracted for reasons of political strength and alliance. In more recent times, immigration to a place of safety, to avoid oppression, or to avoid the military draft are more common reasons for a marriage of political convenience.

Marriage for convenience is a broad category that includes many specific purposes for marriage. Obviously, marriages of convenience provide practical solutions to real problems of the individuals involved. In most alliances of convenience there is no highly emotional attachment to one another when the marriage begins. But the lack of intensive involvement in each other does not preclude the possibility of a good marriage—at least for them. Such marriages can remain stable and strong relationships apart from the ideals of romance and intimacy so long as the marriage remains "convenient" in some way to both partners. When convenience factors are lost, such marriages can become drab cages of empty togetherness.

Spiritual Marriage

For centuries people in most cultures have affirmed the existence of a spiritual component in human beings, even though this component has not been easily defined or readily understood. Various cultures had their own word for the "spiritual" part of a person; the Hebrews used the word *nephesh* (meaning "breath") and the Greeks used the word *psyche* which can be translated "mind" or "soul." In recent times people in western cultures have been turning to prayer, meditation, parapsychology, holistic health and even a regimen of exercise and diet in order to get in touch with their inner selves and discover a deep sense of peace.

In a secular sense, a spiritual marriage is one in which the partners' innermost selves meet and relate. The partners feel that there is a part of themselves that transcends ordinary thought and daily external activity; they may speak of themselves as receiving "good karma" from each other or "being on the same wave length." In a religious sense, church people have often used the word *sacrament*. The word comes from early church history and generally has meant "a visible sign of what is invisible." During the Middle Ages the Roman church extended its control over marriage, first by calling marriage a sacred union and then by requiring marriages to be performed in the presence of a priest; later the church required ceremonies to be conducted inside a church or cathedral. It was then but a small step for the church to declare marriage a sacrament, that is, a divine creation, and as such could not be dissolved.

Most of us would not speak of our marriage as a sacrament, but we would have no quarrel with the view of marriage as a "sacred union." We may speak of ourselves as having a "sacred relationship" or claim that we exchanged "sacred vows" on the day of our wedding, having made our vows in the presence of God as well as invited witnesses. There is a sense in which God's Spirit dwells in the two bodies and two minds that compose a marriage, thus effecting a special unity of purpose and commitment. Admittedly, this is a mystery. But this is exactly how Paul speaks of marriage when he speaks of the mystical relationship between Christ and the church (Eph. 5:32). Exactly how God invades and unifies a Christian marriage will remain a mystery, but, seen from a human perspective, all of God's dealings with human beings and in the world of nature are no less mysterious.

Couples with strong faith in the Judaeo-Christian tradition work hard to keep their marriages intact. They display perseverance and may accept frustration, unhappiness, even cruelty. Prayer is a common means of dealing with marital conflict among devout Christians. Divorce for such couples is not considered a valid means of resolving problems and, in fact, real or even contemplated divorce may induce strong guilt feelings. Obviously, the spiritual marriage has a dynamism that is not easily destroyed.

Romantic Marriage

During the Middle Ages, while the Roman Church was making marriage a sacrament (though at the same time elevating celibacy to a higher plan), a second tradition arose—the tradition of courtly love. Courtly love introduced the idea of romantic love to Western culture, a movement that seems to have been first popularized by the troubadours of southern France and spread through the royal courts of England, France, and Germany. Beginning in the thirteenth century, nobles and knights became obsessed with the idea of serving a noble woman. This woman was almost always married or given over to vows of chastity. Since this beautiful, chaste, and ideal woman was unavailable sexually, love was manifested as an idealized nonsexual love. There was little contact between the noble and the lady. Since neither was seen in an ordinary, everyday light, each resorted to fantasy about what the other ought to be like. The principles of courtly love were embodied in such medieval romances as Cervantes' Don Quixote, the allegorical "Romance of the Rose," and the true-life story of Frenchman Pierre Abelard and his lover Heloise.

The ethic of courtly love elevated the status of women. But the higher status was double-edged, for it required a woman to be noble, pure, and helpless, requiring a knight in shining armor to assist her. This courtly love ethic implanted the ideal of romantic love in our culture. While the notion of romantic love remained outside of marriage during medieval times, it has in modern times become a ruling factor in dating and marriage partner selection. As such, many engaged people carry into marriage notions and expectations based on this romantic ideal.

Romance is idealized love—love with all the warts and wrinkles removed from the intimate relationship. Romantic love usually means being in love with love, being enthralled by those intense, erotic feelings that are perpetually exciting. So intense is the feeling that one cannot function normally; there is little desire to eat, sleep, or concentrate on work responsibilities. The only important thing is being in the presence of the loved one and if not in his/her physical presence then certainly by presence in thoughts. A romantic love affair usually begins by being mesmerized by another's face or body. The strong physical attraction then leads to (or might even begin with) a fantasized exaggeration of a person's intellect, poise, or skills. In romantic love, attraction and intensity of suffering grow stronger when the couple must be separated or when there are barriers to being together. Such a romance grows passionate (remember that the word *passion* comes from the root "to suffer") when erotic desire is thwarted by such obstacles as rejection and opposition by one set of parents, illness, work commitments in separate cities, military service or other call of duty, lack of money, conflicting religious traditions, or even being married to someone else.

We all know that infatuation, genuine flattery, passion, and heart-warming affections are delightful human experiences. And we all know that many couples enter marriages primarily for romance. We know that when couples marry with such romantic attitudes that they may one day wake up and complain that "the glow is gone" or "there is no romance left in the marriage." "The honeymoon is over" has become a cliche among those of us who have experienced the sudden demise of a romance "too hot not to cool down." Being in love with love is not the same phenomenon as being in love with a person. And to place a marriage partner into the mold of some idealized god or goddess is to place a burden on the relationship that is onerous to bear.

Marriage For Companionship

"Only an animal or a god can live alone," Aristotle is quoted as saying. And he appears to be right. Intimacy is a primary human need. There are several studies which show that loneliness may be correlated with disease, death, and suicide. Loneliness is a terrible specter to face. The importance of intimate relationships, even if they never reach their potential in emotional satisfaction, may hold unhappy marriages together indefinitely. Whereas purely romantic marriages thrive on ecstasy and passion, marriages for companion-ship are dispassionately practical. In a companionship marriage the emphasis is on compatible ideals, mutual interests, and shared responsibilities. The marriage is regarded more as a partnership than as an intense romantic relationship.

A companionate marriage places a high premium on the equality of the partners involved. Married couples therefore become comrades in a real sense and will stand by each other against the world if need be. For companionate couples, romantic moments and sexual ecstasy are less important than their deep friendship. Having a mate to talk with, to listen to, to laugh and cry with, and to care for is a high priority which becomes even more important as the couple grows older. As the two age, the marriage continues to provide an emotional support and security based on equality, mutual respect, and deep commitment. This has probably been true from earliest times. The book of Ecclesiastes, written centuries ago, suggests an important truth:

> Two are better than one; they receive a good reward for their toil, because if one falls, the other can help his companion up again; but alas for the man who falls alone with no partner to help him up. And, if two lie side by side, they keep each other warm; but how can one keep warm by himself? If a man is alone, an assailant may overpower him, but two can resist; and a cord of three strands is not quickly snapped.

(Ecc. 4:9-12)

Most of us find our strongest bonds of friendship in marriage. These bonds can be forged from love, attachment, loyalty, or guilt. Regardless of their source, they are extremely powerful.

Companionship marriages are usually sound ones. True friendship in a marriage can be an exhilarating and liberating experience, because friendships cannot be prescribed by institutions or by law, only by the two persons involved. As society has become more industrialized and bureaucratic, it is increasingly within enduring relationships that people expect to find companionship and intimacy, a "haven in a heartless world." The paradox is that even companionship marriages when neglected may drift to the point of providing less nurturance and intimacy and that either or both partners may look outside the relationship for excitement.

An Exercise For The Two Of You

We said at the outset that these categories of marriage were rather general and it is true that our marriages include, to varying degrees, elements in each of the four views. Take time to answer on paper or orally in the presence of each other the following:

1. Which of these views predominated in your thinking when you decided to marry?
2. Cite the ways in which the other three reasons for marriage played a role in thinking about marriage.
3. Often couples who have been married for several years will change their views of marriage. A changing attitude is related to maturity, advancing age, personal or family crisis, or personality and character growth. In what ways have your personal views about marriage changed since your wedding day?
4. Do you perceive that your partner has a different perspective about marriage and, if so, how can this difference be the

11

stimulus for a growing, dynamic relationship rather than an angry, conflict-ridden one?

Scripture

Wisdom builds the house, good judgement makes it secure, knowledge furnishes the rooms with all the precious and pleasant things that wealth can buy.

(Prov. 24:3-4, NEB)

Chapter Three

What Is Marriage?

Before we discuss practical issues in Christian marriage, it seems important for us to state a theology of marriage.

We all know of young people who seemingly rushed into marriage not understanding much of their motivation for mate selection, filled with illusions about the glamor of married life together, and almost fully ignorant of the foundations of a successful marriage. Perhaps you feel that this describes how your marriage began! I got a chuckle out of the description from one marriage counselor, Russell Dicks, of the plight in which many clergymen find themselves:

> "Assuming that sexual expression is irresistible, like a flood, many couples inevitably find themselves standing before a minister to be married. Minister: 'Do you take this woman with all her immaturity, self-centeredness, nagging, tears, and tension to be your wife, forever?' The dumb ox, temporarily hypnotized by the prospect of being able to sleep with her every night, mumbles, 'I do' Then the preacher asks the starry-eyed bride who is all of eighteen, "Do you take this man, with all his lust, moods, indifference, immaturity, and lack of discipline to be your husband, forever?' She thinks that 'forever' means all of next week, because she has never experienced one month of tediousness, responsibility, or denial of her wishes, so she chirps, 'I do,' in the thought that now she has become a woman. Then the patient minister parrots, 'By the authority committed unto me as a minister of Christ, I pronounce you man and wife . . .' As he does, he prays a silent prayer for forgiveness, for he knows he lies. They are not now husband and wife and he knows that few of them ever will be. They are now legally permitted to breed, fuss, bully, spend each other's money, and be held responsible for each other's bills. It is now legal for them to destroy each other, so long as they don't do it with a gun or a club. And the minister goes home

wondering if there isn't a more honest way to earn a living."

Most of us have wrestled with the ordinary questions about marriage. What is marriage anyway? Are marriages made both in heaven and on earth? What steps or rituals must a couple go through in order to be married? How much informed consent is necessary for marriage to take place? What if someone is pressured or coerced into marriage? Would sex relations plus a desire to be married and share life together sufficiently constitute marriage? Put another way, must there be a wedding ceremony and a duly completed and filed marriage license? Is there any value to wedding ceremonies being conducted in a church building or chapel?

Some of these questions may seem to be easily answered, as you know, but others of them are not so easily answered. Regardless, for those of us married already the questions may seem more academic than practical. Thus we will not feel compelled to provide a thorough answer to each question. But it does seem important for us to state a brief theology of marriage and such a statement may well point the way to answering some of these questions. Our only concern here is with the uniquely Biblical perspective on marriage.

We might begin by stating what marriage is *not*. Marriage is definitely the intention of God for most people in normal circumstances. Apart from some exceptional statements by Paul in First Corinthians, directions emerging both from Paul's perspective on ministry and from unique historical conditions, the Bible everywhere underscores the validity and value of marriage. But Christian doctrine has never held that marriage is the ultimate goal of human life or that it is or can be the end-all and be-all of human existence. The Bible presents marriage as a merciful gift of God, a lifestyle that must not be forbidden as evil (I Tim. 4:1-5). Yet the Bible nowhere teaches that a single person is not a whole person, else Jesus as a model human would not be whole. The New Testament views marriage as a union terminated by death (Mark 12:25 and Romans 7:1-3) and in his radical call to discipleship Jesus teaches that the demands of God are always to take precedence over the demands of marriage and family life (Luke 14:20 and Mark 3:31-35). In other words, the ultimate meaning and foundation in life reside in our relationship to God our Father through Jesus Christ and there is no other value and no other relationship in all of humankind which is more important than this vertical relationship.

This leads us to state the basic premise of Christian marriage. *The only valid reason for marriage is to glorify God and to honor the lordship of Jesus Christ.* Thus marriage is not an end in itself. Two people who are contemplating marriage might ask themselves such questions as: Will this marriage honor the lordship of Jesus? Since we are unique creatures called by God to trust and participate in his working in our lives, are our reasons for marriage adequate expressions of the unique purpose of God for our lives? Do we believe that God wants us to share our lives fully with each other? Or can we honor the lordship of Jesus more by being single or by delaying a decision about marriage? Has God called us to be married? Will we be able to use the gifts God has given us as individuals in this marriage? Will this marriage enable us to love and trust and serve God or will it be a handicap to such commitment?

At first thought, this premise and these questions may seem too idealistic. After all, you might be thinking, only a religious fanatic would think to ask such questions. And who could answer them objectively anyway? Our self-justifications and our rationalizations always distort our assessments of ourselves and our purposes, especially when we are convinced that we are in love. You may reflect on your own days of courtship and recall that such questions were at best only on the periphery of any serious thought about a marriage commitment. But it is not too late to adapt these questions to your present situation. You might ask, for example: How can our marriage now honor the will of God? How can our marriage now develop the unique gifts that God has given us individually or as a couple?

As you know, there always seems to be serious re-evaluation of the purpose of marriage and its value as an institution. Divorce rates seemingly are ever increasing. There is an old saying that if people would not marry for such trivial reasons they would not be divorcing for such trivial reasons. To understand more fully how marriage fits into the plan of God for our lives, it is instructive to return to the Biblical narrative of creation.

After God had made the world and all the creatures which were to inhabit the earth, he pondered the plight of the man he had created. John Milton observed in one of his tracts that "loneliness is the first thing which God's eye named not good." Throughout sacred history God has spoken many words of mercy but the first word of mercy ever spoken is one that God speaks to himself as he muses over his creative activity: "It is not good for the man to be alone. I will make a helper suitable for him" (Genesis 2:18). Thus from the beginning of time God has decided that we should not be to ourselves in the world but that we live our days in relationship.

You know well the Genesis accounting of the creation of woman as a special companion for the man. "Male and female created he them" (1:27). Genesis does not tell us that God created man as husband and wife but as male and female, thus enabling a sexual distinction in unity which forms the larger backdrop for marriage. Thus marriage goes back to God's beginning with the human race, something which cannot be said of church, politics, society, or law. Whether or not there is a related ceremonial or institutional procedure in this first marriage is immaterial to the purposes of the historian. But the writer does tell us that God deemed marriage to be an important relationship, for which even family ties will be broken ("therefore shall a man leave his father and mother and cleave unto his wife") and that marriage is to be a lasting union as the two become "one flesh," entering into a deep and unbreakable unity.

God's purpose in your marriage is realized when you and your mate are truly companions to one another. The Hebrew text is perhaps best translated "helper meet," meaning that the woman God created for Adam was given to be a complement, a counterpart, or a companion suitable for him. The "helper meet" for man is more than someone who is able to divide the laborious chores of life for him or to handle half of all domestic responsibilities. She is someone to share his life, his hopes, his dreams, his successes, his failures, his disappointments. You would likely agree that the most difficult thing in the world to do is to live alone. Likely you have become aware of a great need for one person who shares with you a continuous personal history, who is committed on more than a temporary basis to travel the same road in life. This commitment to join hands and venture out in faith, to share the future together, to take the risks and enjoy together the rewards in the unpredictable years ahead, to be full companions who love and trust God to work out his purpose in your lives—such is the basis of marriage.

The marriage relationship of lifelong companionship is founded on the ideal of total commitment. Nietzsche once defined people as animals who can make promises. Of all the living creatures that God has made, only man (man as male and female) is a promise-making, promise-keeping, and promise-breaking being. This is part of the agony and the ecstasy of being human. We as people make sacred covenants because we trust ourselves to keep them, because we trust a higher power for help (as Christians we have the model of perfect covenant-keeping by God the Father and his faithfulness enables and inspires us to be faithful), and because we trust that the person we make promises to is also worth trusting. The pain we feel when promises are broken is the price we must pay which is inherent within the blessing we experience simply because we have the intellectual and emotional capacity to commit ourselves to one another. Do you recall that Paul compared marriage to the relation of Christ with his church (Eph. 5:31-32)? Even though we may be unfaithful to Christ, the Lord has totally committed himself to his body of believers, pouring out his life for us even before we came to love him and promising to be with us always.

Thus Christian marriage is committed marriage. There is an unreserved dedication of your entire self to the survival and growth of the relationship. This is a radical approach to marriage, so at odds with the non-Christian approach to marriage where commitments can be conditional. But a standard which makes radical demands can also be a standard which brings radical blessings and rewards and, in the case of Christian marriage, is pointing to a radically different center in which to find meaning, unity and direction—namely, the Person of Jesus Christ and the empowering of his Spirit.

When Christians marry they say in essence to each other, "We are going to maintain and enhance this marriage relationship no matter what!" What else is the meaning of the vow: "for better or for worse, for richer or for poorer, in sickness and in health, and forsaking all others"? Again, the Lord himself is our model in convenanting. When Christ promised "I will be with you always, even to the end of the age," he provided, in effect, a model for the kind of unreserved commitment that you have made in marriage.

Back to our question: What is marriage? If you were to consult a sociologist you might locate a definition which reduces all conceptions of marriage to common elements, such as "marriage is the socially permitted cohabitation of male and female;" such a definition seems cold and formal. Or one sociologist defines marriage as consisting of "a relationship in which two or more persons maintain ongoing expressive (including sexual) and instrumental (including economic) exchanges"—a definition which seems fair enough except that it does not and cannot state the dynamic of Christian marriage.

A distinctly Christian conception of marriage includes foremost the notion of one man and one woman covenanting a permanent relationship of intimate companionship and personal growth, at the same time making this relationship subservient to their individual commitment to Jesus Christ as Lord of their lives. As the two pledge their love and fidelity to each other they have also united in their pledge to accept the will of God for every area of their life together. In this chapter we have employed the word covenant. The marriage pledge is more than a contract; the motion of contract connotes a lifeless, legal document. The idea of covenant is a living, personal, heart-felt and even sacred pledge between two parties, supported and nourished by mutual respect and love, fidelity and trust.

Thus Christian marriage means two people becoming a sacred

unity—two bodies becoming one with one Spirit (the Holy Spirit) living in them. Christian marriage is "one new life existent in two persons." At its very core, Christian marriage is not simply a matter of finding the right person—it is *being* the right person. And to be that right person one must be rightly related to Christ both as Savior and Lord and also listening to the direction of the Spirit in the Word. As Christians, it is our faith that God works within our marriages; that is the unseen and unmeasurable dynamic that secular marriage manuals ignore. God's Spirit gives us direction both for our marriages and for all our human relationships. If we believe also, as the Scriptures teach, that God is a sure defender and our rock and our fortress, then God in some way lends us his power through Christ to hold fast to our commitment. Of course, all commitments made by humans are tainted by sin, failure, and weakness. But marriages built in faith upon the rock of divine enabling and divine precepts do not crumble as easily as those built upon the shifting sand of human loyalty.

There's one remaining question which might be answered: Just when are two people married in God's sight? What does God join together? Of course, a wedding ceremony is not a marriage and, as Clinebell has so aptly stated, the *fact* of marriage is not the same as the *process* of marriage; in other words, there is a point at which you are married in fact but as you live with your mate you are always in the process of *becoming* married. The question here can lead us into a hornet's nest of controversy that must be avoided here. But the issue is a real one. For most of you, a commitment to a life-time relationship was the same as "getting married." But some of our children may not make the same connection and you may know that "living together" has become a fast growing trend among college-age young people in the last decade or so.

We must concede that while the Bible is concerned about the state of matrimony, nowhere in the Scriptures do we find any concern about the role and nature of a ceremony. There is no moral law that tells us how we must begin a marriage. There is a theology for marriage; there is no corresponding theology for marriage ceremonies. Marriage is an invention of God while wedding rituals are inventions of various cultures. In Old Testament days, a young man and young woman (take, for example, Isaac and Rebekah) would only have to be introduced as mates selected for each other, look longingly into each other's eyes, go off together into a tent, and make love; in that culture, the two then would have been considered married. Customs have changed, thankfully. As for the process of becoming married in fact, I would suggest the following three steps:

1. COMMITMENT made mutually to one another for life ("till death do us part"). Feelings about commitment may emerge gradually during courtship, but sometime before real marriage such a mutual commitment is made explicitly and almost always made verbally.

2. COMMUNICATION of the commitment is made to appropriate members of family, friends, and any interested parties. A public announcement or public declaration and affirmation (such as in the legal records required by law) are highly expedient if not essential to the fact of marriage. I would not contend that God requires this kind of public declaration and legal accounting, but both common sense and the Christian sense of responsibility dictate it. First, a duly recorded document of wedding ceremony and marriage contract provides legal protection of the partners involved in the relationship. To other people you are relying on the force of the law to say "hands off my mate," both literally and figuratively. Second, a public declaration and record of marriage provide protection for any children born to the union who, of course, deserve the right to legitimate status.

You will likely agree that sexual union does not make two people married to each other. If a man and a woman sleep with each other without telling society that they are doing so, they may consider themselves many things, but they cannot consider themselves *married.*

3. CONSUMMATION or sexual union, the two becoming one flesh, is essential to the fact of marriage. Herein, there may be some rare exceptions in certain medical or physiological cases (and, of course, some would cite the marriage of Joseph and Mary as a reality before intercourse, but their marriage was the only one of its kind). I do not believe that one is married in the ideal or complete sense until after the fact of this physical union—a union which has symbolic significance because it is representative of the spiritual and emotional commitment already made.

Prayer In Duet

Dear God, our Father, thank you for giving the gift of our marriage and for your blessing upon our union. As we strive to be truly one with each other, please enable us to be one with you and your Son as Lord of our daily lives. Adapting the words of your great apostle Paul to the Galations, may we be able to say: "We are crucified with Christ and we no longer live, but Christ lives in us. The lives we live in the body, we live by faith in the Son of God, who loved us and gave himself for us.'' God, help us to discover ways that the promise of Jeremiah for the future can become, in our lives, a joyful reality in the present: ". . . there will be heard once more the sounds of joy and gladness, the voices of bride and bridegroom, and the voices of those who bring thank offerings to the house of the Lord, saying, 'Give thanks to the Lord Almighty, for the Lord is good; his love endures forever.' '' Through Jesus, Amen.

Chapter Four

Why Did You Marry?

We dare to suggest that you may not have married your mate for the reasons you thought you married.

Have you ever sat in your Sunday School class or in some other group setting, looked around the room at the people present, and wondered how and why various couples ever married? "I wonder what he saw in her?" "I can't for the life of me figure out how those two ever got together!" "As college homecoming queen she could have any man on campus, but why did she pick him?" We've all heard statements like these, and perhaps we have often made similar remarks ourselves.

More importantly, you may have questioned the reasons for your own selection of a mate. Why did you marry your mate? If you had the decision to do over again, would you make the same selection? And what determined the time in your life that you would marry? If you had delayed five or ten years, would you have married the same person? Do you feel that you are the same person now that you were when you were married?

The question of "who marries whom" is one which has aroused scientific inquiry as well as common sense. The common sense answer may seem paradoxical: we all have heard that "opposites attract," but it is also logical to accept the old cliches about "like marrying like" and that "birds of a feather flock together." Actually, both polar positions in this folk wisdom could be true; it all depends on the characteristics being considered. If by "like" we mean social characteristics such as ethnic origin, age, race, religion, vocational interest, social status, and residential location, then the view that mates then tend to be alike (homogamous marriages) is so true. If, however, we refer to psychological traits, attitudes, tendencies, or needs, then a description of marital harmony is by no means simple.

Why did you marry the person to whom you are committed? We have all viewed each other through an initial screening or filtering process that dealt with our "field of eligibles." For most of us, certain people were screened out as ineligible for consideration. But then, either rapidly or quite deliberately, you settled on the one person who was right for you. Most of you would say that, whether through the providence of God or through fate, your paths crossed and, inexplicably, love developed between the two of you. As your love developed and deepened, you moved toward the decision to spend your lives together. You might concede that the need for security and satisfaction at various levels of existence entered into your decision.

We say that persons "marry for love," but we are too intelligent to believe that love is some mysterious force that strikes indiscriminately. The experience of "falling in love" is a common one, but it is also a baffling and esoteric phenomenon. We can describe the behavior of a person who is "falling in love" and "falling out of love," but we are unable to explain *why* the chemistry flows or does not flow between two people. Love is related to a lot of factors and we would be wise to reflect on the deeper reasons which explain our love-decisions.

Our choice of mates was determined as much by feelings as by facts and as much by unconscious factors as by conscious factors. This may come across as disillusioning, but it must be stated: many of us were not aware of the major determinants in our mate selection. And furthermore, the fate of a marriage may well have been decided before the wedding occurred. The human psyche is formed early in childhood and the result is enshrined in the person, often without his conscious awareness. Marriage does not create anything new in the personality of the partners. So, then, one partner might choose another in order to repeat the patterns of childhood and adolescence behavior and conflict.

You and your mate may have longed for the kind of support and gratification that you could get only in consort and traditional commitment with each other over a long period of time. Yet as your marital system developed its own rules, customs, agenda, expectations, and interactional style, which *are* your relationship, you find that the longed-for happiness and gratification do not ensue or are only marginal. You may find yourself providing a source of more unhappiness and frustration for the other than a source of happiness and gratification. What is happening? Well, not only are you changing as a person (or failing to change as a person when your mate is changing), but it is possible that those unconscious and hidden determinants of mate selection are now obviously coming to light and influencing your marital fulfillment.

Does this destroy the conception of marriage as a free and rational choice? Perhaps so, or at least it may be saying that we make marriage choices for less than rational and logical reasons and that our perception of ourselves and potential mates is distorted. If we are hoping to aid troubled marriages we need to know why mates select each other and this kind of self-knowledge is not easily attained. Psychoanalysts contend that, when marriages founder, it is usually not because the couple has incompatible interests but because they are ignorant of the unconscious purposes that determined their respective choices. Santayana described the process of falling in love as "that deep and dumb instinctive affinity."

Consider the fact that neurotics marry neurotics. Then, quite understandably, neurosis is carried over into the marriage and the same neurotic patterns continue either in harmony or discord. This can be illustrated several ways from real life. Mates often unrealistically hope that the other partner can handle for them the difficult situations, real or imagined, that induce anxiety. A shy person who fears abandonment may marry an extrovert, seemingly at ease in all social situations, but who also fears abandonment; the complementarity is only on the surface and it cannot supply the desired support. A husband who feels the need to exercise power and authority (perhaps partly ingrained in him by Biblical indoctrination) falls for the woman who will be a wife in "total subjection." That wife may need a man who will direct her every step. One mate may not want to mature intellectually or emotionally and may find a mate who will not want him/her to mature. A person may choose a partner to hide some real or fantasized fault. A woman may marry a man who will protect her from the real world and maintain her sense of security. Patterns get entrenched and the possibilities are numerous. It may be said that all marriages are mixed in some regards.

One psychologist, Joel Block, has addressed this theme of the complex process of choosing a marital partner: "Few of us marry out of mature love. We marry out of hope, and we hope that our fantasies will spring to life. We dream of love, but developing a loving relationship is another matter. Marriage, involving two complex and everchanging adults and, in most instances, one or more equally complex and rapidly changing children, precludes continuous and perfect harmony. . . . A man may want a hostess, a mother, an accessory, a centerfold, a sister, a slave, or a tyrant. A woman may crave a father, a son, a savior, an escape from home. . . . [Although it is possible] to achieve a reasonably nurturing, loving, and workable relationship despite the inherent flaws of the institution, most marriages, unfortunately, do not achieve this; they are more often characterized by discord and destructiveness."

All of us are familiar with the marriage contract. Written marriage contracts have existed throughout the history of man's civilization and there are some extant marriage contracts that may be dated five centuries before Christ. Your own contract may be framed and displayed or it may be stashed away in a wedding photo album or file cabinet. The marriage contract is a legal document which sanctions and protects personal and property rights of marriages, traditionally to the advantage of the male. But such legal documents are only a small part of the overall concept of marriage contracting.

In marriage enrichment, it might be helpful to think in terms of the marriage contract—not the legal one filed with the court clerk but the unwritten "contractual dynamics" that are powerful determinants of the behavior of both parties and the quality of our marriages. The individual contract is a person's expressed and unexpressed, conscious and beyond-awareness concepts, of his obligations within the marital relationship and the benefits he/she expects to receive in return (note the reciprocal nature of the contract). The nature of individual contracts is determined by deep needs and wishes that each expects marriage will fulfill. These will include healthy and realistically plausible needs, as well as those which are neurotic and conflictual. Each spouse may be only remotely aware of the terms of the other's contract. When significant aspects of the contract cannot be fulfilled, as is inevitable, and when these lie beyond his/her own awareness, the disappointed partner may react with rage, injury, depression, or withdrawal, and by provoking marital discord by acting as though a real agreement has been broken. This response is aggravated when the spouse believes he/she has fulfilled his/her obligations but the other has not. Sometimes it is a real challenge even for a therapist to determine some of the more deeply buried obligations of the unwritten contract. And yet, when clarification of the contract occurs there may be a dramatic improvement in the couple's relationship and the growth of each partner. We need to listen carefully to such statements as "I've been giving good quantities of X and Z in this marriage, but I get no A in return—all I get is a little of B and C." Such statements reveal much about individual contracts and hidden agendas of marriage expectations.

This would be a worthwhile assignment for all of us who once said "I do." Sit down with pen and paper and compare a list of the reasons why you selected your mate. Can you discover less than wholesome and mature reasons? Neurotic or shaky reasons for marriage and mate selection would include the need to build self-esteem, the desire for "legalized" and guilt-free sex, the fear that your man or woman was the last possibility for marriage, the desire to get away from home or school, some fantasy that marriage will end all personal problems, the need to have someone tell us what to do, strong parental pressure or rebellion against same. Would any of these apply in your case? Then answer: do you think the reasons for which you married are still valid for continuing your marriage? Was or is there a hidden agenda of expectations in your marriage relationship? Are you willing to make that agenda of hopes and expectations clear to your partner? Can you list more valid and deeper reasons for continuing your marriage that did not exist in the early months and years of your union? Such soul-searching is never easy, of course, but it can yield rich benefits to your union.

Prayer

Father, marriage was given by you and blessed by you throughout the ages in order to enrich our lives. Marriage is both mysterious and sacred—but surely not so sacred and mysterious that it is exempt from rational scrutiny. Search me and know my heart-felt motives for every decision I've made affecting this marriage. Purge me of any unwholesome habits and attitudes that led me to select my mate so that our commitment for the present and for the future may be rooted in our mutual growth, realistic commitment, and renewed faith in the possibilities that lie ahead. Through Jesus. Amen.

Chapter Five

Are Enduring Marriages Happy Marriages?

Let's look at several types of enduring marriage and then attempt to state some qualities of a happy marriage.

Are you happy in your marriage right now? If you answer affirmatively, would you say that you are very happy, moderately happy, or only slightly happy? Have you been happier with your marriage in the past than you are right now? Does it feel good to you to be a husband or wife? Do you feel that you are living with a friend, someone you like and trust in every way and someone who returns this fondness and trust? Is it fun and exciting to be in the presence of your mate?

If you believe that your marriage is a very happy relationship, and if you can answer "yes" to the last three questions, then for certain you are living in a nurturing relationship. If you have children and they share the same joy and excitement of being in your family—the sense of being among true friends—then all of you are living in a nurturing family. If you answer "no" or "not often" to the same questions, if you do not consider yourself to be happy in marriage and you wish you were single again, then you are living in a troubled marriage. Every marriage can be placed on a scale from very nurturing to very troubled.

How would you define a happy marriage? Would it be a marriage where quarreling and conflict are virtually non-existent? Is it a marriage where the emotional needs of each mate are satisfied? Is it a marriage where there are several children to share in the joy of living? Actually, we are going to find that defining a happy marriage is no easy task. For example, one reason that a couple may have few arguments and conflicts is that they do not talk to each other very much. The fulfillment of needs is important in happy marriages, but sometimes the ego satisfaction is linked to unrealistic and neurotic demands on the other. And paradoxically marriages seem to give the most satisfaction when there are no children present; in other words, children and marital happiness *seem* to be opposed to each other (several studies reach this dismal conclusion). But let's not place blame directly on the children. Children per se do not cause the loss of marital fulfillment, but the circumstances under which we must raise them in contemporary society (the financial burdens of childrearing often meaning dual-worker families and less time for pleasures and the responsibilities of parenting; the new parental roles that children create; the increasing burden of decision-making and the balancing of values necessary as children move into adolescence). We must add that while the marital relationship may be less fulfilling in the presence of children, there may be a trade-off for many couples who find fulfillment in their parental roles.

When we turn to the Bible for instruction on happiness and fulfillment in marriage we will soon discover that we are at a distinct disadvantage. The Bible does not talk about qualities of an enduring marriage per se. In fact, the Bible gives us no pictures of the interior of a marriage; there is no role model for marriages today. We cannot know what it was like in the marriage between, say Isaac and Rebekah, Joseph and Mary, or Moses and Zipporah. Of course the Bible in its ethical teachings has much to say about relationships and as we read narratives of the intimate friendships of David and Jonathan or Ruth and Naomi we learn something of what makes a relationship strong and satisfying; but even here there are few role models.

Another way of looking at marriage is not in terms of happiness, but in terms of stability. What we find is what many of us know already—there is often little correlation between happy marriages and enduring ones. Some happily married couples may undergo a crisis and break up; many unhappily married couples choose to stay together. In recent years a number of sociologists have explored some of the diversity in outwardly conventional marriages. One of the best known and most frequently quoted studies is the one completed by Cuber and Harroff. These researchers discovered that there is a great range of marriages and that marital happiness and satisfaction are not necessarily important aspects of all these marriages. As I state the five basic types of marriage they identified, consider which type best describes your marriage:

1. *Conflict-Habituated Marriage.* This form of marriage may be described as the "Who's Afraid-of-Virginia-Woolfe?" type of marriage. Conflict is its most distinguishing characteristic; the couple simply fights with each other often. Such couples need each other for sparring partners, so they fight and fight and fight, often bruising each other physically or emotionally. However, they do not believe that such continual fighting is grounds for divorce. The fighting is usually discreet, rarely taking place in front of others outside the

family; therefore, few outside the family group may know about this conflict and hostility.

2. *Devitalized Marriage.* This type of marriage is one that started with a great sense of romance, vitality, excitement, and mutual identity and pleasure, but as the years pass the couple drifts apart. Whatever time the two spend together is "duty time," whether they entertain, take the children on vacation, or meet social responsibilities. Yet the two get along amiably and do not contemplate divorce.

3. *Passive-Congenial Marriage.* In this third type of marriage, the couples differ from the devitalized couples in that they were never highly emotional about each other to begin with. Couples begin these marriages with low expectations which change little over the years. Partners do not gain much satisfaction from each other, but they view being married as a comfortable and convenient way to live while directing true interests and creative energies elsewhere. For the husband, work and male companionship may be very important; the wife gain her satisfaction from her children, her friends, and her career if she has one. Although such a utilitarian marriage does not measure up to romantic ideals or develop multifaceted intimacy, it is satisfying—at least for them.

4. *Vital Marriage.* In the vital relationship the couple not only spends a lot of time together, but enjoys being together. The lives of the two are closely entwined with respect to matters that are important to both of them. Togetherness brings excitement, satisfaction, pleasure (One man said of his wife: "The things we do together intrinsically are not fun—the ecstasy comes from being together in the doing"). Partners in vital marriages engage in church and social activities like everyone else, get involved with their children like everyone else, but they privately maintain a strong, positive emotional bonding.

5. *Total Marriage.* The total marriage is similar to the vital marriage, except that the husband and wife share in more aspects of life together. There is almost total involvement in the lives of each other. For example, the wife may be involved in various ways in her husband's work. In the past, husbands and wives have worked together in the making and sales of crafts, operating a store, running a profession, and in research and counseling.

What these five marriage types have in common is that they are all enduring. They do not represent degrees of marital happiness and satisfaction, although it will be obvious to you that the vital and the total marriage types conform more closely to our traditional images of what marriage is supposed to be.

Marriages are really quite varied. If your marriage is one which is enduring until one of you dies, then that is good; that is what God intends for you. But whether your marriage is happy or unhappy may well depend on your subjective evaluation of your life together. Partners give their own particular meaning to marriage. And our family background serves as a crucially important factor determining our evaluation of happiness in our marriage. The home in which we were raised provides a strong model for what we come to expect in our own marriage. Researchers have concluded that young people are usually conditioned early in life in ways that will make them good or bad risks for marital happiness. Several circumstances are predictive of a happy marriage:

1. Superior happiness of parents
2. Childhood happiness
3. Lack of conflict with parents
4. Home discipline that was firm but not harsh
5. Strong attachment to mother and father
6. Parental frankness about matters of sex
7. Premarital attitude free from disgust or aversion toward sex

Happiness in marriage usually comes from a "habit of happiness" that was developed by each partner before marriage. Children from happy homes, children who have seen happiness and fulfillment in the lives of their parents and who have experienced happiness in relationship with their parents, have a tremendous advantage in developing a happy marriage. If your parents modeled for you a devitalized or even conflict-habituated marriage, there are important odds stacked against your marital happiness—but the barriers are not insuperable. As Christians, we may confidently hold that we have the help of God and his Spirit to provide the instruction and resources to make our marriages strong and happy.

So let's aim for deep levels of satisfaction and fulfillment in our marriages. Would this not be God's will for our lives lived together? What is your vision for your marriage? Just because researchers have concluded that the vision of the happy, satisfied, open, companionate, and loving marriage for a lifetime is an elusive, romantic ideal for most people does not mean that we as Christians should scale down our expectations. Why should we not desire relationships, in or out of marriage, that are marked by unselfishness, kindness, generosity, affection, truthfulness, affection, mutual concern, and good manners? Do we not see enough cruelty, meanness, selfishness, deceit, coldness, and ill will in the rest of life? Perhaps this is the issue for Christians—we can ask that our marriages and our family life become an emotional and spiritual oasis in a world where all other human relationships are more greatly tainted by sin and are more likely to be characterized by brokenness, selfishness, coldness, and wavering commitment. Is there any reason why our marriage and family life cannot be the closest thing to "heaven on earth"?

Exercise For The Two Of You

Below is a listing of some characteristics of a happy, satisfying, fulfulling, and nurturing marital relationship. Though the lising is not exhaustive, take the time to see how many of the characteristics describe your marriage.

1. Relationship is motivated principally by the pleasure of the other person's presence and not by his/her function.

2. Conversations are personal, connected, and engaged in easily and spontaneously, no conscious self-censorship or concern about avoiding certain subjects, being misunderstood, or saying something better left unsaid.

3. Partner is best friend and if he/she were not your mate you would desire this person for a friend anyway.

4. Energy and good feeling experienced in the presence of mate.

5. Celebrations and events are continuously created and experienced according to inner feelings rather than the demands of ritual and social pressure.

6. Laughter is easy and spontaneous, not based on jokes or "making each other laugh," but rather on shared perceptions and shared values.

7. A feeling of being listened to and understood.

8. All feelings, even negative ones, are expressed easily.

9. Joy felt in the presence of the children.

10. Capacity for playfulness and spontaneity in both sexual and nonsexual behavior.

11. Members of the family all touch one another and are openly affectionate.

12. People are silent or they eat, drink (or watch television, read novels, romances, and magazines, etc.) because they have chosen to use time at home in that way rather than because of a need for numbing or escaping from the here and now.

13. Little blaming and fault-finding between partners and family members.

14. Fights focus on the real issues in the conflict and when completed leave each partner with the satisfying experience of feeling more known and real to the other.

15. Absence of intimidation; neither partner afraid of the other.

16. Energy is concentrated on the relationship rather than energy concentrated mainly on situational aspects of marriage such as the house, social responsibilities, desires of children, etc.

Prayer In Duet

Save us, Dear Father, from the folly of expecting the rewards and happiness of marriage without the labor and pain; and from the carelessness which, knowing what is necessary, neglects to do it. As we treasure our mutual love and our shared lives, make us zealous in guarding them from all danger and decay. Through Jesus. Amen.

Chapter Six

Is Your Marriage Holy Wedlock
Or Wholly Deadlock?

Now let's state some symptoms of a troubled marriage.

John and Letha Scanzoni tell the story of a publisher who felt considerable embarrassment over an incident a few years ago. Seems that the publishing company had issued some full-color posters to illustrate a series of religious-education materials. But through some oversight, two picture captions were reversed and the miscue was not noticed before orders were shipped. A picture designed to illustrate marriage was labeled "John the Baptist in Chains." And the picture of the fettered wilderness preacher was entitled "Marriage."

No doubt the mix-up seems appropriate to a lot of people. Men especially have been known to speak of marriage as a kind of bondage. Some have drawn comparisons between the wedding band and the tourniquet (both "cutting off circulation") and others have emphasized the word *lock,* as in "chains of wedlock." In more recent times, large numbers of women have complained that marriage is a trap, locking them into conventional roles which preclude full development as achievers and as persons. Dissatisfaction in marriage has been called "the seven year itch"—it is an indication that the couple's original reasons for marriage no longer seem valid to them and their marriage has lost its meaning.

Little wonder then that the question has been raised: "Is there life after marriage?" *Life* suggests energy, vitality, movement—just the opposite of what is motionless, inert, or static. But the static model for marriage is unrealistic. Recall at the first of this book our assertion that all marriages were moving in *some* direction, either toward greater meaning or fulfillment or toward stagnation and death. Hopefully, the previous chapter and this one will lead you to consider carefully the direction your marriage is moving, however slowly and subtle the movement.

If you take your marriage commitment seriously you will not find the subject matter in this chapter to be very pleasant. Perhaps, and hopefully, you will not find your marriage described in the next listing; but you may find some of these marriage traits among couples you know and love. Have you seen those little pamphlets informing all of us of "Seven Danger Signals of Cancer"? The purpose of listing these signals, of course, is to alert us to danger while successful treatment is still possible. This is analogous to what I hope this chapter might accomplish for troubled marriage. When couples experience their marriages only as an unexamined drift through personal history, every day seems like the previous day, that is, until something "suddenly" happens. A wife "suddenly" asks for a divorce. A husband "suddenly" runs off with a younger woman. One spouse "suddenly" deserts the other. But such "suddenlies" are unrealistic! Those who experience such shocks have neglected to see the signposts. They have neglected to deal constructively with the challenges that each of them confronted with the mere passage of time. In fact, the only alternative to a "suddenly" in a neglected relationship is for the marriage to become an empty shell of physical proximity.

Have you ever known anyone well who has experienced the breakdown of a marriage? If so, you know that for months after the end of the marriage the events and developments leading to its breakdown are likely to occupy the thoughts of the separated wife and husband. Over and over they review what went wrong, regret or justify their actions, consider and reconsider their own words and those of their mate, ponder again the advice on which they acted or failed to act. Continuously they replay actual scenes in their minds and create scenarios that did not happen but could have happened. As the scenes of a disintegrating marriage are replayed, they are enabled through the vantage of hindsight to see clearly the signals of failure and relationship disaster to which they were so blind earlier. (Incidentally, all of this rumination leads to the formulation of an *account,* a personal narrative of the marriage failure, which focuses on what each partner did or failed to do; additionally, it allocates blame among the self, the spouse, and any third parties or forces which may have entered their lives, and so settles the moral issues of the separation. Never mind that the account is not an objective and impartial record, assuming that any such account could be constructed; the account enables the person suffering to work through the grief and anxiety therapeutically.)

Following are seven symptoms of a troubled marriage. The symptoms are indicative of an *emotional* divorce, whether or not a *legal* divorce confirms and announces the alienation. Please note that this is not a complete listing of trouble signals and also that there is considerable overlapping in this listing. Separately, but especially together, these symptoms spell the need for immediate marriage therapy.

1. The loss of interest in sexual relations is an obvious symptom of a troubled marriage. Of critical importance here is the symbolic meaning of a sexual relationship. Sexual union is symbolic of emotional and spiritual union. Sexual accessibility implies a kind of emotional accessibility. Waning interest in sex suggests a loss of physical attractiveness that once was the mate's, which, of course, may well be the case; or, lack of interest may suggest that the husband or wife is sexually inadequate. Regardless of the proper interpretation, the loss of interest in sex signals trouble.

2. A lack of genuine communication between husband and wife is another danger signal. Some couples seemingly lose their ability to talk to one another; instead they fuss and bicker during the rare moments that interrupt an apathetic silence.

3. The third symptom might be called the "empty house syndrome." The house is empty because the various members of the family choose to be away from the house most of the time except when eating and sleeping. No matter what else enriches their lives— warm friendships, notable achievements at work, competence in sports, pleasurable hobbies—people caught in an unhappy marriage tend to feel isolated and beset. In the troubled marriage, one or both partners may have more fun *away* from the mate rather than *in* his/her presence. If one of them has enjoyed a good day at the shop or the office, the anticipation of spending an evening in strained silence almost makes returning home a chore.

4. Fights over every conceivable difference of opinion and value constitute another danger signal. Fights will vary from marriage to marriage, but may be sudden and violent, and thus shattering to the emotional equilibrium of each partner, perhaps raising doubts about his/her sanity, frightening to both and further alienating each from the other.

5. Another symptom of troubled marriage is when repressed anger is channeled into attempts at rational discussion, but the discussion is distorted by dwelling on the negative aspects of the relationship. Certain themes seem to recur in such discussions: "This marriage was wrong from the start." "I never really loved you to begin with; furthermore, you never really loved me—we only thought we were in love." "Look at all the years we have lost." "If we were to end this marriage, it would only be rectifying an error we made a long time ago." Such self serving statements set the stage for rationalizing the termination of the marriage.

6. When a critical spirit pervades the marriage we may know that

marriage is troubled. Likewise when both publicly and privately a husband or wife is treated with scorn and disrespect or when criticism and manipulation are the most commonly employed methods of changing the behavior of the other. Because a marriage can end as a result of verbal abuse and psychological violence, we might keenly observe the spoken, body, and sign language of emotional divorce. This language translates something like this: "How do I resent thee? Let me recite the ways. And what I can't tell you I will demonstrate by lack of trust, lack of conversation, intimidation, nagging criticism, humiliation, refusal to listen, rejection, interrogation, lack of consideration, manipulation, domination, jealously, and possessiveness." Overstated, for sure! But undoubtedly such behavior is present in one form or another in troubled marriages.

7. The last symptom we cite is more subtle: a troubled and floundering marriage succumbs to numerous temptations for minor betrayals. Some examples: siding with a child in the child's dispute with a husband or wife; reporting confidential information about the marriage to third parties in violation of the mate's wishes; refusing to accompany the mate to a social event given by the mate's friends, colleagues, or family (or attending but acting immaturely); responding with blame rather than comfort and reassurance to the spouse's recounting of a disastrous day. Of course there may be large betrayals, too, notably sexual infidelity.

An Exercise For The Woman

Below is a list of personality traits of unhappily married women. Make a notation beside each trait which you think applies to you. (This list and the one for men following are from a study by Lewis M. Terman.)
1. Characterized by emotional tenseness.
2. Inclined toward ups and downs of moods.
3. Give evidence of deep-seated inferiority feelings to which they react by aggressive attitudes rather than by timidity.
4. Are inclined to be irritable and dictatorial.
5. Have compensatory mechanisms resulting in restive striving, as evidenced by becoming active joiners, aggressive in business, and over-anxious in social life.
6. Strive for wide circle of acquaintances; are more concerned with being important than being liked.
7. Are egocentric.
8. Have little interest in benevolent and welfare activities unless these activities offer personal recognition.

9. Like activities fraught with opportunities for romance.
10. Are more inclined to be conciliatory in attitudes toward men than toward women.
11. Are impatient and fitful workers.
12. Dislike cautious or methodical people.
13. Dislike types of work that require methodical and painstaking effort.
14. In politics, religion, and social ethics are more often radical.

An Exercise For The Man

Below is a list of personality traits of unhappily married men. Make a notation beside each trait which you think applies to you.
1. Are inclined to be moody and somewhat neurotic.
2. Are prone to feelings of social inferiority.
3. Dislike being conspicuous in public.
4. Are highly reactive to social opinion.
5. Often compensate for a sense of social insecurity by domineering attitudes.
6. Take pleasure in commanding roles over business dependants or women.
7. Withdraw from playing inferior role or competing with superiors.
8. Often compensate by daydreams and power fantasies.
9. Are sporadic and irregular in their habits of work.
10. Dislike detail and methodical attitude.
11. Dislike saving money.
12. Like to wager.
13. More often express irreligious attitudes.
14. More inclined to radicalism in sex morals and politics.

Scripture For Meditation

The fifth chapter of Proverbs is a warning about the defilement of a marriage relationship. When Solomon warns of sexual infidelity, he shoots straight. Solomon concludes his warning with gentle counsel about the blessing of exclusive love with the mate of our earlier years:

> "Drink from your own well, my son—be faithful and true
> to your wife. Why should you beget children with women

of the street? Why share your children with those outside
your home? Let your manhood be a blessing; rejoice in
the wife of your youth. Let her charms and tender
embrace satisfy you. Let her love alone fill you with
delight.''

(Living Bible translation)

Chapter Seven

Are You Really In Love?

Before we continue to discuss practical aspects of marriage, we need to make certain that we understand the Biblical meaning of love.

What would you say is the most important element in the success of any marriage? You would likely say that it is love. You might believe that real love is the main reason for marriage and, in the lyrics of a Sinatra hit of the 50s, "love and marriage go together like a horse and carriage." One problem we have when we talk about love is that the word "love" has too many meanings. Surprisingly, the English language does not provide a larger vocabulary for dealing with the subject. Eskimos have several words for snow because the varieties of snow are important in their daily lives. Likely you have heard that the ancient Greeks had three words for love: eros (sexual or physical attraction), philos (brotherly), and agape (spiritual). But we rely on the one word "love" to carry the load of numerous and varied meanings, values and experiences.

The feeling of love is a powerful emotion and at times it seems that how love happens and the extent of the feelings cannot be understood by anyone, including the person who is experiencing it. You may believe that love will be a transforming experience, recognizable as unique and different from any other emotional experience or feeling in the past. Then there are times when you wonder if you can identify your feelings accurately. Even after you talk about and try to analyze the components or dimensions of love, it is often such a subjective set of overwhelming feelings that efforts at description seem incomplete and inadequate. The belief that if you have to ask what love is or how you know if you are in love, you have never experienced it is a belief which speaks much truth. So powerful and overwhelming are the associated emotional and feeling experiences that psychologist Abraham Maslow describes the feeling of love as a peak experience. Can love be defined and analyzed? Our purpose here is to state something of the true nature of love from the Christian perspective.

What is love? Thus far we have spoken of love as a feeling. And love is a feeling, but it is much more. Love has to do with sentiment, yet it must transcend sentiment. The meaning of love has varied with the many cultures and the many ages in which humans have lived. For several years I have relied on a statement by Harry Stack Sullivan for the definition of love: "When the satisfaction or the security of another person becomes as significant to one as is one's own security, then the state of love exists." Smiley Blanton has written: "True love between a man and a woman may be defined as a relationship in which each helps to preserve and enlarge the life of the other. Such a love presupposes in both a maturity of emotional expression, free of childish compulsions to exploit, to dominate or to destroy. . . . Mature love thrives therefore on a realistic basis of equal exchange which sets up a benign circle of mutual pleasure, reassurance and inspiration." And, of course, the most sublime statement on love is the love poem of I Corinthians 13.

Love is learned behavior. People are born with the capacity for all kinds of social learning, and thus they must learn to love just as they must learn to hate. Several factors contributed to our learning to love. After birth there are bonds of attachment. When one creature makes repeated efforts to gain and keep the proximity of a certain other creature (we use general languge here since attachments occur in nonhuman creatures as well as in people of all ages), he/she is attached to that creature. When the attempts are mutual, there is an attachment between the two. Now attachment is a part of love—a basic, essential part, but not all of it. God has equipped a newborn baby for building an attachment to the mother who, in turn, is especially equipped to build an attachment to her baby. In the early months of life, babies tend to obey and cooperate with the people to whom they are attached; thus, we can see the origins of respect, one of the elements of love. As the early years pass, the child establishes bonds of attachment to father, siblings and other household members, other kinfolk and friends. From some of the family (especially grandparents), the child may learn unconditional love. And by the time a person can become a committed member of a pair, he/she has piled up a great deal of experience in interpersonal relationships. Within the context of various attachments, he/she has cared for other people, respected them, responded to them, taken responsibility for them, and sought to know and understand them. For one reason or another, there may be faulty or inadequate learning and the child grows up having difficulty establishing and maintaining love relationships.

While we speak of learning love it should be pointed out that God himself is the perfect teacher of love, not so much through what our

Father has said as what he has done. God's steadfast love for Israel, his chosen people, never wavered despite Israel's unfaithfulness. The enacted parable of Hosea is most instructive on God's love. And God's love for all of us was dramatically demonstrated at Calvary. "Even for a just man one of us would hardly die, though perhaps for a good man one might actually brave death," states Paul; "but Christ died for us while we were yet sinners, and that is God's own proof of his love towards us" (Rom. 5:7,8). Because God's love comes to us, we are enabled to demonstrate a measure of agapic love toward others. It is through such love that we as humans partake of the divine nature.

Others factors contribute to our learning to love. Love, with its emphasis on ego needs, is probably more important and more basic to the American culture than to almost any other culture. To be unloved in this culture is to be more than unwanted—it is to be unchosen, to lack importance in the eyes of a significant other. This is extremely unsettling in a culture where so many personal products are advertised with links to love relationships and romantic involvement. Pop art does its share to pressure people into falling in love. Do you remember the once-popular song "You're Nobody Till Somebody Loves You" or John Lennon's lyric "All you need is love; love is all you need"?

As modern culture pushes us toward falling in love, our views on love become distorted, soft, and sentimental. Sensuality, sexuality, attraction, and adventure often pass for love. And many people see the problem of love primarily as that of being loved rather than that of loving or of developing the capacity to love. Pop culture impels people to develop marketable love qualities—the right amount of education, special talents developed, stylishness in dress and grooming, use of the right personal products, and ownership of the right material possessions which are displayed with class. Then the person with these qualities goes into the marketplace as a nice package to barter for the best possible package in exchange. Of course, there is some validity to claims that beauty and health will make a person more fall-in-lovable, but it is rather far-fetched to say that a particular toothpaste or cologne will make you irresistible to the opposite sex.

Love between a man and a woman can and should be, according to John Powell, the most liberating, maturing, and fulfilling experience of adult human life. But this kind of profound relationship from which great blessings flow is not easy to achieve. Powell points out that counterfeit versions of love are frequently accepted for the real thing:

1. The physical conquest. Herein, one or both of the partners sees the other primarily as a source of physical, sexual pleasure. The partner is "used," perhaps even willingly and without deception, as a source of sensual pleasure. Do you remember the uproar when the world's best known religious leader declared that lust was possible *within* a marriage? We could debate whether lust is possible within marriage, but there can be no doubt about the possibility of abuse in marriage when the partner is viewed only as an object, not a subject.

2. The psychological conquest. The conquest here is much more subtle and complicated, but it is a conquest nonetheless. A partner can be seduced psychologically, to get him/her to fall into love, to fall at the feet of the conqueror, to be dominated and submissive, not just as a body but as a person. The partner becomes a trophy to the ego of the conqueror.

3. The projected image. Herein, the person is in love, not with the person as he/she actually is, but with a projected image of who he/she should be. The image may be derived from a mother, father, or dream. The person may place unrealistic expectations on his/her mate and never come to know the mate as a real person.

4. Infatuation. This term refers to a temporary state of being in love. It implies deception, or that the relationship is and will remain shallow, and thus is doomed. There is no doubt that much infatuation passes for real love. Apparently, when individuals are going through the emotional relationship, they call it love; when it is over, they call it infatuation. By calling past love relationships infatuations, the person maintains the uniqueness of love, so that when he/she falls in love at some future time, the term "love" will refer to the new, not the used and inadequate.

5. Romance. Romantic love is based on a complex of values, beliefs, and attitudes that have been handed down for centuries in the Western world. Falling into this counterfeit version of love is beautiful, wonderful, mysterious, incomprehensible and ever magical. Recall the old hit by Johnny Mercer and Harold Arlen, "That Old Black Magic":

That old black magic has me in its spell
That old black magic that you weave so well
Those icy fingers going down my spine
The same old witchcraft when your eyes meet mine. . . .
For you're the one that I have waited for,
The mate that fate had me created for.

Romantic love is blind, thriving on a reality distorted by beautiful clothes, makeup, moonlight, candlelight, firelight, no light, perfume, music, exotic places and enchanted evenings. Of course, all marriages thrive on the romantic dimension but romance alone is counterfeit love.

Psychologist Abraham Maslow analyzes love in terms of two categories: Deficiency-love and Being-love. Deficiency-love is basically selfish, based on needs that the other person can fulfill. The other person is frequently regarded as an object. A man may love a woman who gratifies him sexually, glories in *his* achievements, is subordinate and dependent, turns to him for guidance and advice, takes care of his needs (his cooking, laundry, etc.). A woman may love a man who provides for her, satisfies her sexually, makes all important decisions, is smart, makes life adventuresome. The man may say, "Yeah, Rosie, she's a good little wife" and the woman may say, "Yeah, Hank, he's a good provider for the family." In this kind of love relationship, the two do not relate to each other as individuals who are growing, but as roles, objects, and functions.

Being-love, by contrast, is love for the very being of the other person. Such love is given without any desire for reciprocation, although this kind of love is usually reciprocal. Being-love involves a depth understanding and appreciation of the significant other in a person's life. A person does not love another in order to feel good or to gain status among peers but out of the joy of personal and relationship growth. Being-love can encompass the whole spectrum of human emotions—boredom, fear, anger, grief, compassion, sympathy—without being endangered. This is the kind of love which produces marriage enrichment with the passing of years.

How can you know if your love attachment is counterfeit or real, if it is neurotic or healthy, if it is genuine or hypocritical? Take a close look at your marriage relationship. Do you grant your mate the right to be an independent individual in any meaningful sense? Do you feel the need to control your mate or be controlled by your mate? Do you see in your mate someone who will never say no to you, who will do your every bidding without complaint and, hopefully, fulfill your every need? Do you see your mate as someone to take over your life completely and absolve you of all responsibility to think and make decisions on your own? Do you see your mate as a mother-substitute or as a father-substitute? How these questions might illuminate the interior of your marriage should be obvious. Rollo May has described a non-growth marriage when he noted that "it not infrequently happens that two persons, feeling solitary and empty by themselves, relate to each other in a kind of unspoken bargain to keep each other from suffering loneliness."

Let's continue our remarks about love with four important statements.

Statement One: LOVE IS NOT A FEELING.

So you remember the popular song "Feelings"? Feelings are important. Feelings may indicate the beginning and continuation of true love. But love is neither established nor maintained by feelings alone. Feelings may be compared to yoyos, up and down, depending on such fickle and unpredictable matters as the temperature, amount of sunshine, hormones, the amount of sleep a baby got, the time of month, the friendliness of the last phone call.

There are lots of good feelings and exhilirating times in a genuine love relationship. But over the long-haul of a life-time commitment there are more than just a few bad feelings. The flux of love—the oscillation between attraction and repulsion—is a normal part of every marraige. A fully committed man will occasionally be infuriated by his wife and vice versa; but neither reports temporary frustrations and trifling complaints to anyone but the other. In the course of a love-relationship, two people may have to go through a winter of emotional discontent to find a renewal of love in the springtime. The growth of love is based on deepening understanding and this may come after running the gamut of negative emotions.

Statement Two: LOVE IS A COMMITMENT, AN ACT OF THE WILL.

The commitment to have a loving relationship with another person is one of the most important decisions of your life. "Love is an activity, not a passive effect," states Erich Fromm; "it is a 'standing in,' not a 'falling for.' " Christian marriage affirms that love is a conscious decision to yoke yourself with another person through thick and thin ("in sickness and in health, for better or for worse, etc. . . ."). In the marriage ceremony the minister does not ask "Do you love this person?" He asks *Will* you love this person?" The Christian faith teaches that loving is something you can decide to do. You can will to love. The basis for your marraige is not so much your feeling but your promise.

In excusing his infidelity, many a man has said, "I just don't love my wife anymore." This statement is a denial of the commitment that he made at the moment of marriage. It works as rationalization for the man/woman who believes that love is only feeling. You realize, of course, that it is crucially important that you do not offer a commitment of love that you are not able or willing to honor. Inexperienced and immature people tend to do this and, we might add, at the cost of risking tremendous shock and inflicting deep wounds to another.

Statement Three: EFFECTIVE LOVE IS UNCONDITIONAL.

There is no third or middle possibility—love is offered either unconditionally or with conditions. To the extent that conditions are attached ("I will love you when . . . until . . . after . . . as long as"), effective and true love does not exist.

Your love should lead you to say in essence to your mate: "The gift of my love means this: I want to share with you whatever I have that is good. You did not win a contest or prove yourself worthy of this gift. It is not a question of deserving my love. I have no delusions that either of us is the best person in the world, or that we are necessarily best for each other. The point is, you have chosen me and I have chosen you and together we can make it."

The essential message of unconditional love is this: "You can be your best self and not worry about losing me. You can express all your thoughts and feelings with absolute confidence. You do not have to be fearful that love will be removed. I cannot always predict my reactions or my strength, but one thing can be known—I will not reject you or forsake you."

Unconditional love is an ideal that only God can live up to perfectly. We have cited already the demonstration of God's love while we were yet in sin. We might commend ourselves for our capacity for steadfast love, but actually unrequited love is not as common as we might think. Unrequited love usually fades away, though not without pain. Many popular songs deal with the sadness of one who has loved but is no longer, such as the classic "Smoke Gets in Your Eyes." Sadly, many people renege on love commitments when they themselves have not been totally betrayed or abandoned, head to divorce courts, try to fall in love again with another (fallible) human without ever relying on the help of God, challenging their ingenuity, relying on personal resources, or testing coping mechanisms. Relying on what Bonhoeffer called "cheap grace," they excuse themselves to others, declaring, "Oh, God's great forgiveness will take care of me." Generally, love works only if we will work at it. Most who fail are those who never made a strong commitment to succeed.

Statement Four: LOVE'S ROLE IS GIVING AND SHARING.

Love and labor go together. If you love, you are in a constant state of active concern with and for the loved person. There are three dimensions in this giving and sharing:

A. Affirmation. A sense of his/her own worth is the greatest gift that you can give to another. ("You are a unique, unrepeatable and even sacred mystery of humanity.") This affirmation is liberating. God loves us but he gives us freedom to be ourselves, to choose. A love that clutches and clings and attempts to control the object of the emotion is not love as much as it is the expression of neurotic needs and pressures.

B. Awareness/Alertness. Your sensitivity to the needs of your mate is essential. But needs are constantly changing. Your mate must be constantly watched with a look of love, not out of jealousy, but in an effort to learn and respond to needs. Alertness certainly involves listening, for as Paul Tillich said: "The first duty of love is to listen."

C. Activity. This means doing things WITH and FOR your partner. Rollo May, in *Love and Will,* states, "The opposite of love is not hate. It is apathy." Love will not allow the loving relationship to be neglected.

As we have noted, true love preserves, enlarges, and bestows freedom to the life of the other person. The all-absorbing love that puts a person so completely in the clouds that he/she fails all courses or loses a job lacks some essential ingredients of love. For love does not make either the giver or recipient less active, less effective, less fully functioning; rather it promotes growth and increases awareness of meanings, needs, and opportunities in the world about you.

In conclusion we might ask if there is a link between the love of God and the love of humans? First, let's do away with the notion that only Christians can truly love. Non-Christians, by God's common grace, are capable of genuine loving relationships and, in fact, many Christians are quite adept at non-loving (or apathy). But the confessing Christian finds it easier to love others because he/she has first been loved by God. As you capture something of the essence of God's love you are empowered to love others. Love is not merely "one of the fruits of the Spirit"—it is first and foremost of the fruit of God's Spirit (Gal. 5:22,23).

God gives his love to others through the love that you give to them. You are a mediator of the love of God. God loves others through you and me and others feel the force of his love as we demonstrate our love to them. Love is not optional for Christians. It is the distinctive sign of discipleship: "By this shall all men know that you are my disciples—if you have love for one another."

Prayer

Thank you, O Lord, that you did not love us simply in some abstract or philosophical sense, but that you demonstrated your love in such a dramatic and costly manner at Calvary. Through your grace and by your enabling may our love commitment to you and to one another grow stronger and dearer as the years go by. Through your only Son, who taught and lived the meaning of perfect love, we pray. Amen.

Chapter Eight

How Much Equality Can Christian Marriage Stand?

We now dare to offer a brief statement on the controversial issue of authority relationships in Christian marriage.

Are there politics in your family life? You might recoil at such a question. After all, you might reason, intimate relationships are based on love alone. But the politics of family life—who wields the power, who calls the shot, who is expected to do what—can be a miniaturized version of the same complexity and explosiveness of politics at the national level. In the average family there can be coalitions, civil wars, coups, revolts, truces, diplomacy, even secessions. The exercise of power is often subtle. There are a few marriage manual authors who out-Machiavelli Machiavelli with their counsel on how to get what you want out of your husband or wife.

Most likely you would prefer to think of your marriage and family life not in terms of politics but in terms of authority relationships. The issue raised here is an important one for Christian marriages and, as you know, there has been no little amount of debate, both in public forums and in living rooms and dens across the country, on this issue. As a Christian you want to make certain that your authority relationships meet Biblical standards but, at the same time, you may be troubled by several blunt statements in the New Testament about wives being in submission to their husbands in all matters.

You would certainly agree that authority must exist in the home. You would also agree that the line of authority between parents and children is quite clear. Authority between you and your mate is another matter. Is there any place for the concept of obedience in a husband-wife relationship? Perhaps the best that can be said for obedience is that it is not a popular notion in marriage. There have been occasions when fulfilling the role of officiating minister for weddings that I have been earnestly requested to delete any reference in my remarks or in the vow to be recited to wifely obedience. Apparently, a vow to love and cherish is quite enough for many young Christian brides.

Two views *seem* to be in opposition. The traditional view emphasizes Paul's declaration that "the husband is the head of the wife as Christ is the head of the church." The traditionalist interprets this to mean that the wife can make only such decisions as her husband allows her to make, but in all matters the husband commands unquestioning obedience. A traditionalist might speak of a hierarchy of power or a chain of command: CHRIST

HUSBAND

WIFE

It seems that much of the newer material on this subject being produced by Bible-respecting authors does not emphasize the idea of authority and obedience, but it does tell wives to be submissive and states that husbands should be leaders rather than authoritarian figures.

The modern view is influenced, undoubtedly, by the various liberation movements of the twentieth century. Modern theorists forward a strong argument by suggesting that marriage as an institutional system is dying and is being replaced by a new companionship form of marriage. It is true that marriage has always been a flexible institution which reflected the needs and values of the particular time and place of various cultural sections. In contemporary society, people do not need to be married in order to populate the earth. Nor does a man need a wife and several children for economic reasons. People are not driven to marriage by their relatives, by necessity, or out of a sense of duty; single people are no longer considered odd, deprived, or deficient. The main if not sole reason for marriage in contemporary society is for companionship. And companionship marriage has two main characteristics—love and equality. This modern conception of marriage holds that the husband and wife are co-equals and co-creators, sharing in a fully equalitarian relationship. All major decisions are made after mutual consultation and consent. Each partner has the power/authority to make decisions that solely affect him/her. There is an emphasis on mutual submissiveness—each defers to the other in the area of the other's responsibilities and expertise.

Which of these positions best describes the authority relationships in your marriage? Which of the two is closest to the Biblical standard? At this point I offer two observations:

First, the view that you pay lip service to may not be the view that you and your mate actually live by. The husband who sits in a Bible class and barks loudest to his peers about his God-given authority and right to command obedience (perhaps "amened" by his wife) may be the most pusillanimous ("henpecked") man in the community. Remember that authority is based on law of one kind or another while power is based in personality. A strong, dominant woman is likely to exercise power over a weak, passive male simply by the force of her personality and temperament.

Second, when people are honest, they must admit that each family works out its own system of decision-making between the husband and the wife and any children living at home. And what works for one marriage may not work in another marriage. Often the pattern of decision-making in a marriage is never clearly stated or even understood by the husband or wife. Virginia Satir believes that analysis of many families is like opening a can of worms, a worn expression, to be sure. The can of worms is all entangled with worms writhing and squirming; they really can't go anywhere except up and down, around and sideways, with no sense of purpose or direction, but they certainly give the impression of aliveness. Do you agree that this is the way many families conduct themselves? Have you ever stopped to analyze the family relationships in your home? Who is in charge? What are the roles assumed by each member of your family? Is there an influence on your family decisions from a person outside the family or a former family member?

If you refer to the Scriptures to support a viewpoint on this issue, please examine and interpret any text in light of its historical and cultural setting. The concept of submission is taught most clearly in two passages:

(1) I Peter 3:1-6. This epistle was written during a time of religious persecution; consequently, there were many religiously-split marriages. There was deep concern over how a Christian wife could convert her heathen husband. Recall that both the Greeks and the Romans taught the unquestioned obedience of the wife and the full right of husbands. In fact, older human cultures were authoritarian and hierarchical; it was believed that horizontal relationships were too dangerous and that only vertical relationships could be trusted to hold communities together. In essence, Peter is saying to his female readers: "You sincerely want to convert your husbands. Instead of preaching or nagging, follow the Old Testament pattern of modesty, submissive behavior, and a meek and gentle spirit. This is nonverbal evangelism and is an effective strategy, even if your husband does not now believe the word."

(2) Ephesians 5:21-25. This passage is one of the most important statements about marriage in the New Testament. As with the previous text, this passage is set in the traditional context of the ancient Near East. Neither from a religious viewpoint nor from a pagan viewpoint was any new dogma forwarded in Paul's declara-

tion: "Wives, submit to your husbands" (vss. 22 and 24). Such counsel could be heard everywhere in the ancient world. And Christian women would not have taken this command to be absolute. They would have known that it did not mean for them to worship their husbands, to obey them unquestioningly, or to elevate them to the place of God. Rather, they would have taken this command to mean that they must act toward their husbands as all the believers would act toward Christ—in faithfulness, in service, in honor, in devotion, and in love—because what wives do to their husbands, they are in fact doing to Christ. If a wife is unfaithful, hostile, complacent, nagging, or inconsiderate toward him, she thus treats her Lord.

What is unique in this Ephesians passage is that Paul lays the groundwork for an altogether new ideal of marriage—marriage may be understood as the picture of the relationship between Christ and the church. In the Old Testament era, a woman might be commanded to submit to her husband because she was of less value than he. Now the husband is to treat his wife as an equal, loving her as he loves his own flesh. Husbands must serve their wives as Christ served the church, emptying themselves in sacrificial devotion akin to Christ's. The passage begins with a command to both husbands and wives: "Submit to one another out of reverence for Christ" (vs. 21). In other words, we may say that both husband and wife are to submit to one another. And while we may scripturally sustain the view that the male is the head of the family, that headship is a function only and not a matter of status or superiority. In Christ relationships are restored and renewed so that everyone has the right to full personhood.

What does it mean for the husband to be head of the household? Perhaps the most we should claim is that the husband is the leader in the household, especially in spiritual matters. But to be the leader does not mean to be the dictator. It is a sad situation when the husband expects his wife to perform as a salve. And yet, it is obvious that this dictatorial pattern of authority is not simply a relic of the past. Many husbands are still dictators (e.g. in areas of decision-making about children, money, sex) so that the concept of genuine partnership is absent. How a wife responds to this dictatorship generally depends on her personality and her own expectations in marriage; some women are "bossed" and told to "mind" to such an extent that they become broken persons while others rebel by manipulation, deception, or even by an affair with a man perceived to be more loving and considerate of personal wishes and feelings. How many intelligent, resourceful, and energetic women do you think have been made to feel like insignificant, helpless doormats who are incapable of formulating their own views or making decisions for themselves ("I'll have to speak to my husband about this first.")?

> Husband, husband, cease your strife,
> No longer idly rave, sir;
> Though I am your wedded wife,
> Yet I am not your slave, sir.   (Burns)

Christ has never called anyone to be slaves to any person but himself (cf. John 8:36; Gal. 5:1; I Cor. 7:23). This is not to say, of course, that a marriage in which the husband is 100% dictatorial and the wife is 100% compliant will not function. The question is whether or not such a pattern harmonizes with a Christ-like ideal of intimate relationships.

You and your mate might wish to sit down and discuss the implications of all this for your marriage. What place does equality have in your marriage? What does it mean to be free and equal in Christ? How can your lives be structured so that both of you through marriage can fully exercise all your hearts and souls and minds and strength? Is it possible for your marriage to have both submissiveness and equality? I would insist that marriages can be characterized both by submissiveness and by emotional equality. Remember that the principle of submissiveness cuts both ways. There are times that the wife must be submissive to the husband and there may be many times in which it is obvious to the husband that he must be submissive to the decisions and wishes of his wife. Now obviously there may be many occasions in which you disagree as to who ought to be submitting. If the principle of mutual submissiveness seems difficult, you might remember that a relationship between a tyrant and a slave is less complicated than a partnership of equals, just as a dictatorship makes less demand upon intelligence and resourcefulness than a democracy. You will need to be skillful in teamwork, perceptive in terms of who has the greater needs and larger stake to be affected by the decision, and resilient enough to practice the give-and-take of a relationship in which the roles of each may need to change occasionally.

In intimate Christian marriage, equality can be a reality if both of you fully recognize that you are united in your values, needs, and feelings. Equality does not mean a strict and even distribution of household labor, yardwork, childcare responsibilities, and career priorities. In no way can these tasks be divided precisely, even with the legal expertise of a renowned lawyer. Emotional equality is not based on a written contract about who washes the dishes and who feeds the dog. And emotional equality is destroyed whenever one of you says, "I am better than you because I am president of my firm and you are only a homemaker" or "I bring in more money to this household than you."

Emotional equality in a marriage means that each of you takes the other seriously and at face value, accepting all the feelings of one as legitimate and important to the other. It means each of you takes time to really know the other, that each is responsible for establishing intimacy with the other. Intimacy, of course, is much more than a steady sexual relationship, as Thomas Oden implied when he said, "Sexual intimacy without interpersonal intimacy is like a diploma without an education." Intimacy is "shared privacy." Intimacy involves getting to know the partner at various depth levels. It is possible for a man and woman to live together under the same roof, as husband and wife, for many years, to sit together for morning and evening meals each day, to sleep each night in the same bed, and to join their bodies in sexual union—all of this for a lifetime and yet not really know each other as persons. This has, in fact, been true of many traditional marriages. No real intimacy has developed. Intimacy is prerequisite to equality. Specifically, emotional equality means that the husband's disappointment and frustration about his failure to receive a wage increase is not more or less important than the wife's distress over a costly repair and inconvenience in home maintenance. Put succinctly, emotional equality considers the feeling and not the event; it is the necessary ingredient for any union that is deeply human.

Prayer In Duet

Teach us, Dear God, to honor and respect each other, knowing that we are equally precious in your sight, equally called to share the responsibilities and joys of marriage. You have given us minds; may we develop them to their full capacity for understanding and learning and for serving in our world. You have given us hearts for loving; may we exercise forgiveness and compassion toward each other. You have given us bodies; may we honor them and keep them pure and healthy as temples of your Spirit. You have given us strength and moral direction; may we seek fulfillment of your will, supporting one another by our labors of love. In the name of One who, though totally himself, was totally faithful to you as Father. Amen.

Chapter Nine

How Do You Feel About Yourself?

We insist now that your self-concept is an important factor in your marriage happiness and success.

Virginia Satir has made the point that family life is something like an iceberg. She states that most people are aware of only about one-tenth of what is acutally going on in their families—the tenth that they can see and hear—and they often think that is all there is. Just as a sailor's fate depends on knowing about the iceberg *under* the water, so the fate of a marriage depends on understanding the feelings and needs and patterns that lie hidden beneath everyday events in the life of that marriage.

Have you stopped to consider that one very important factor in the success of your marriage is the nature of your self-concept? What do you think of yourself? How do you see yourself in your relationship with your husband or wife and with any children that might be in your family? Do you consider yourself capable and competent in the family roles you have assumed? Do you feel good about yourself? Do you trust yourself? How you answer these questions is important. The wisdom literature of the Old Testament affirms that how we "think in our hearts" determines our reality (cf. Prov. 23:7).

A high sense of self-esteem is one of the greatest contributions that you can make to the relationship with your mate. The great qualities of human character—love, compassion, integrity, empathy, forgiveness, kindness, and responsibility—all flow from a person who has high self-esteem. And these are the qualities which enrich a marriage relationship. In fact, we could argue that you cannot truly love any other person until you have come to love yourself as a person. Recall that Jesus enjoins you to love your neighbor *as you love yourself*. The person whose self-esteem is acutely low can only be grateful to lean abjectly on another. In such a case, the relationship would not be that of a companion but of a servant or protegé.

What happens in a marriage where one or both partners has low self-esteem? (As you read the listing below, do you see any of this happening in your own marriage?)

1. Negative comments carry more weight than positive comments. When someone reviews or evaluates your performance at some length, do you tend to remember and replay the positive or the negative criticism? If you have low self-esteem you tend to focus on the negative criticism. This is true even if you have received far more compliments about your preformance in some area than negative comments.

2. The opinions and evaluations of sources outside the marriage take precedence over personal views and evaluation. While the views of other people are not facts, you will accept unfavorable opinions as facts if you have a poor self-image.

3. Compliments are "played down." If you have low self-esteem you will tend to feel unworthy and undeserving of genuinely offered compliments of your personality and performance. You tend to rationalize in your mind by statements like "That person does not really know me" or "That person is just trying to be kind to me."

4. The messages of other people are distorted. If you have low self-esteem, even the most neutral data may be given a negative slant. A casual statement can be taken as a "put-down." A word spoken in playful jest may be taken as harsh criticism.

5. Harsh self-judgment is a part of thinking patterns of people with low self-esteem. If you have an internal critic who is always condemning you for behavior or attitudes in the past, if you are always recounting your sins of the past despite the fact you have confessed them to God and others and have sought forgiveness, then most likely you have a poor self-image. A poor self-image serves as a magnifying glass which transforms an imperfection or an insignificant mistake into an overwhelming symbol of personal unworthiness. The imperfections and trivial mistakes grow in importance until they dominate your entire reality.

Do you see any implications of this for your marriage? Consider the matter of communication with your mate. If either you or your mate has a poor self-concept, then normal communication between the two of you as adult equals may be very difficult at times. A husband may say, "This den is really cluttered with a lot of papers and magazines" and the only message that the wife with low self-esteem hears is, "As for your performance in housework, you are most incompetent." A wife may tell her husband who has readied himself for a worship assembly, "That tie clashes with your suit," and the husband with low self-esteem hears, "You are incompetent when it comes to selecting your own clothing." The person with low self-esteem seldom finds anything very funny and does not find it easy to laugh at personal problems; consequently, his/her mate may feel the pressure of being on guard always lest some person poking fun be taken as a personal attack.

Our purpose here is not to discuss ways of building self-esteem. Suffice it to say, self-esteem is not part of our genetic endowment—it is something you must learn and maintain for yourself. While your mate plays a big role in determining your sense of self-worth, ultimately you are responsible for personal self-esteem. And if you have learned low self-esteem, it can be unlearned, and something better can be learned in its place.

One beautiful aspect of living the Christian life is that all of us may always rely on God's estimate of us as the major source of our self-esteem. The Bible story of redemption underscores the fact that God created us in his own image, cared enough for us to give moral direction for our lives, and loved us enough to send Jesus to die for us. You must remember that God knows you even better than your mate and even better than you know yourself and that God always renders righteous judgment. Neither your standing before God nor your eternal destiny is determined by your performance in the past, present, or future; what counts most is your grateful response of trusting faith to his magnificent gift of love and grace.

Scripture And Prayer In Duet

Those who are led by the Spirit of God are sons of God. For if you live according to the sinful nature, you will die; but if by the Spirit you put to death the misdeeds of the body, you will live, because those who are led by the Spirit of God are sons of God. For you did not receive a spirit that makes you a slave again to fear, but you received the Spirit of sonship. And by him we cry, "Abba, Father." The Spirit himself testifies with our spirit that we are God's children. Now if we are children, then we are heirs—heirs of God and co-heirs with Christ, if indeed we share in his sufferings in order that we may also share in his glory.

Romans 8:14-17

Dear God, it's not always easy to walk the tightrope above sinful pride on the one side and destructive feelings of inferiority on the other. Instill in us a deeper sense of your steadfast love for both of us so that we may have a deeper appreciation for who we are as your children and what we may become as joint-heirs with Christ, your Son. And because you have affirmed us in so many ways, most of all at Calvary, may we always be alert to the opportunities to affirm each other through expressing appreciation, encouragement, and affection. Help both of us to stop being our own ultimate judge and jury. May the good feeling of being loved and accepted fully by you give us complete liberation to love and accept not only each other, but all members of our extended family and all other significant people who share with us in the living of these days. Through Jesus. Amen.

Chapter Ten

Are Men And Women Different?

We dare to jump into the hornet's nest of controversy over the issue of sex differences as we seek to understand what it means to be male and what it means to be female.

You may have heard the old riddle that purports to dramatize a trait in our culture: a young boy has been seriously injured in an automobile accident. He is bleeding badly and needs immediate surgery; his father has already died from injuries in the same accident. The injured boy is wheeled into the operating room for surgery and the tall, handsome surgeon with white hair is summoned to his side. The surgeon looks at the boy and incredulously exclaims, "This is my son!" Question: Who is the surgeon? The riddle plays upon age and sex stereotypes. The surgeon is the boy's mother. We do not expect this because the clues given (tall and handsome rather than petite and beautiful) set us up to imagine a male. We traditionally think of surgeons being male and we expect mothers of young children to be young themselves and expect them to be at home caring for the children.

All cultures classify people by sex and age, but assumptions about traditional sex and age roles are increasingly being challenged and altered. Are men and women innately different? If so, how? Obviously there are biological differences between male and female which all of us would celebrate as a part of the Creator's grand design? But are there emotional and instinctual differences between men and women? Did God make the woman a more natural parent because she was given a womb and the capacity to carry, deliver, and nurse life? Do her hormones make her naturally more submissive to the male and is the male more naturally suited for a leadership role for reasons not culturally determined?

These issues are hotly debated in both scholarly and popular literature and the ramifications seem to be as political as they are spiritual. There is no way that we can provide answers to all of these questions, but there are some implications that are important for us if we want to enrich Christian marriage experience.

A Brief Glossary

BIOLOGICAL SEX depends on chromosomal makeup, external genitalia, internal genitalia, testes or ovaries, hormonal states, and secondary sex characteristics (such as body hair and voice).

GENDER IDENTITY refers to the psychological state in which the person comes to believe and assert either "I am a girl" or "I am a boy." The first stage of gender development is believed to be complete by about age three.

GENDER (SEXUAL) ROLES refer to the learning, adoption, and performance of socially accepted characteristics and behaviors for someone of a given gender. In each society there are interests, traits, responsibilities, and types of action defined as appropriate for males, others defined as appropriate for females, and some deemed appropriate for both males and females.

ANDROGYNY is derived from the Greek *andros,* meaning "man," and *gyne,* meaning "woman." An androgynous lifestyle is one in which there is no sex differentiation. Men and women are allowed to choose from the full range of emotions and behaviors based on their temperaments and humanity rather than their biological sex.

Let's answer the question raised in the title. Men and women *are* different—"God make them male and female." Men and women are different anatomically, sexually, biochemically, and hormonally. These differences combined with other factors—cultural conditioning or socialization and/or divine ordination and appointment—mean significant differences in mood, sources of self-esteem, role, and image at home. Most of the literature on Christian marriage written by conservative and evangelical Christians seems to support and sanction conventional stereotypes:

Female Role Tendency	**Male Role Tendency**
"Be-ers;" Women prefer the less activist role of homemaker; nurturance and support orientation.	"Do-er;" Men prefer to be achievers; task and power orientation.
Sensitive to feelings of others	Insensitive to feelings of others
Personalizing and subjective	Analytic reasoning and intellectualizing
Emotional	Hides emotion

Easily influenced	Not easily influenced
Noncompetitive and supportive	Competitive and aggressive
Blame internalized; difficulty expressing anger	Anger and blame externalized; vengeance sought
Greater comfort with being touched	Physical distance and aloofness
Gentle	Rough
Feelings easily hurt	Feelings not easily hurt
Difficulty making decisions	No difficulty making decisions
Ambivalent about success in the organizational world	Fear of failure in the organizational world; get ahead at all costs
Communicative	Nontalkative
Exhibit weakness; hide or repress strength	Exhibit strength; hide or repress weakness

By conventional thought there is a subtle difference between the sexes implied in the giving and receiving of gifts. When a man gives a woman a substantial gift, the implication to the woman is that he is willing to take on some form of responsibility. However, when a woman gives a man a substantial gift, she is implying that she would be happy to be his responsibility.

The main problem with this conventional listing is that it is indeed based on cultural and societal stereotypes. After his characterization of a television actress in the film *Tootsie,* Dustin Hoffman said, "I operate like most men. I'm just as perfunctory as the next guy in terms of showing affection. . . . But I know when I put on the woman's outfit, I'm very physical. I go put my arms around them." Of course Mr. Hoffman's experience was personal and subjective, but there are simply too many studies in the various fields of psychology, sociology, anthropology and endocrinology that all point to the same conclusion—despite anatomical and other differences, virtually all the differences in male and female behavior are culturally, not hormonally, determined. Though we are *born* male or female, we *become* "masculine" or "feminine" according to the norms of our society. Soon after birth the human brain takes over and overrides all systems, including the endocrine system. If men are more aggressive than women, for example, it is not the Creator who has made them that way but cultural conditioning (although, we might add, anyone who thinks women are not more aggressive than men has not seen women at the opening of a bargain basement sale!).

This conclusion need not be unsettling to Christians who trust in the wisdom of God. In fact, it should work toward the advantage of stronger and more fulfilling marriages. Nothing in modern research findings compels us to abandon the idea that husbands should assume leadership in the family as both husbands and wives defer to the leadership of the Lord. And certainly no research can destroy the deeply ingrained value that motherhood is a worthwhile investment of a woman's time and energy. And we may continue to hold to the concept that a man and woman should become one flesh, finding their identity in each other rather than as separate, competing individuals. Perhaps now we are in a better position to see that the roles of homemaking, parenting, career-building, love-giving, and problem-solving can be shared more equally among the two who are married to each other.

The Male In Our Society

What does it mean to be a "real" man in America? Bruce Feirstein parodies him in *Real Men Don't Eat Quiche* (1982):
Question: How many Real Men does it take to change a light bulb?
Answer: None. Real men aren't afraid of the dark.
Being male is no easy task. Pride in being male is instilled in young boys to give them courage for the challenges ahead. Despite all the talk about machismo, there is no single image of the "real man" in our society. The entertainment media (even and especially the television commercials) present several distinctly masculine images: the bigshot businessman, the Marlboro man on the prairie, the lover boy moving from one carnal conquest to another, the blue-collar brawler, the jet-set playboy, the tough football player, and hard-working adventurer who looks forward to his "Miller-time." Ideal male roles in our culture consist of certain "core requirements" based on independence, physical strength, courage, and perseverance, thus allowing the man to protect the weaker members of society (eg. women, children, and aged). The "real man" is stoic and seldom reveals his emotions. Machismo is often the attempt by the male not to feel. The phrase "inexpressive male" is used to describe a man who never shows any weaknesses, even with his companions, and

struggles under the added burden of keeping secret his weaknesses, sins, and pains.

These images underscore the stereotypes which in turn have a significant impact on how men feel about themselves. Appearing "manly" can impose a heavy burden of stress and energy. The attrition rate is high for men: more young males die from accident than females; over two-thirds of adolescent suicides are committed by males; three times as many boys as girls are in mental institutions; five times as many boys are arrested for juvenile delinquency; the majority of adult criminals are male; adult males suffer more hypertension and heart failure and have lower life expectancy; more males are alcoholics, drug addicts, and compulsive gamblers. The stoic and traditional male roles can become especially difficult when the man passes 40 and is confronted with body and appearance changes, career stagnation, and drastic changes in his family unit.

The relevance of all this for Christian marriage should be obvious. First of all, power can be a source of difficulty for men as they get older. The male sense of power and control does not facilitate personal relationships. The more a man is absorbed in power struggles, at work or at home, the less energy he devotes to relationships. Genuine intimacy is more difficult for men to achieve than for women. One cannot control another person and at the same time be intimate with that person; thus, notions of home leadership based on power and control must be abandoned. Additionally, men find it more difficult than women to acknowledge a problem in a relationship and seek help. Christian husbands need to be especially aware that the wife is usually the one to seek help first. Men are usually the last to recognize and concede marital difficulty and many adamantly refuse to seek professional help in resolving difficulty.

The Female In Our Society

For centuries there has been no real controversy about defining the role of the woman. Put simply, she finds her total fulfillment in being a wife and mother. The steps toward becoming a "real" woman are described in such books as Helen Andelin's *Fascinating Womanhood* (1974) and involve:

1. Proper attitude (dispensing with any air of strength or ability and adopting an attitude of frail dependency).

2. Ceasing to do masculine work (work that involves strength and muscles; and, if stuck with masculine work, then doing it in feminine manner).

3. Being submissive: always yielding to the husband's rule, opinions, discretion, and judgment.

4. Trying not to excel the husband or other significant men (though some victories in English, literature and grammar are acceptable).

5. Depending always on his care, protection, and courtesy.

6. Allowing fearfulness to continue (as women have a natural fear of dangers, snakes, bugs, spiders, mice, the dark, and strange noises).

7. Employing childlike mannerisms (eg., pouting, crying, sticking out lower lip) to get their way.

You may be smiling at some of the prescriptions or you may be taking most of them quite seriously. If we were to add to the above qualities the features of being young, beautiful, thin, and adoring, then we would conclude that there are very few "real" women in America. The ideal of the "real" woman can place as onerous a burden on women as the counterpart image for "real" men places on men. For one thing, the ideal woman gets older, a natural occurence on which the cosmetic industry thrives. Also, more and more women today are facing the specter of separation and divorce and the subsequent return to the single life. And finally, more women than not will find themselves facing widowhood. So the stereotypes, images, and prescriptions are not always relevant.

While the traditional roles for women have been those of wife and mother, in recent years an additional role of the woman as worker has been added. This new role has had a tremendous impact on family life. In fact, the most basic factor related to the changing nature of the American family has been the changes in the roles filled by women. And most of this change seems to have taken place in the last quarter century. The change has been so widespread that we have generally come to expect that most women will be gainfully employed at various times in their lives. Women tend to work before they are married and, after marriage, will quite often continue working until the first child arrives. Current statistics indicate that about 45% of the labor force are women (as compared with about 20% in 1900). Between 1960 and 1975 married women with children under the age of six more than doubled in rates of labor-force participation.

Have you ever heard preachers and Bible teachers lament the fact that large numbers of women have entered the labor force and accuse these working women of adding pressure to their marriages and neglecting their responsibilities as wives and mothers? Interestingly, a number of studies are showing that women's working outside the home does not conflict with traditional female roles.

To summarize these studies: (1) The employment of the wife does not appear to have a negative effect on her marital adjustment and satisfaction; nor is there much evidence that her employment affects her husband's feelings about the marriage. (2) Working wives continue to do most of the cooking, housework, and childcare; however, they spend less time with these chores than nonworking women. (3) The employment status of the wife has minimal effect on what the husband does in the home. (4) The working woman's day is longer at the expense of her sleep and leisure.

Work does conflict with traditional feminine roles when women choose to enter careers in which they directly compete with men for power, money, and prestige and when they choose careers instead of motherhood. It is not simply a matter of whether or not a woman is working outside the home that influences marital adjustment, but more the extent to which her behavior violates role expectations, whether her expectations or those of others.

We mentioned that being male in our society was no easy task. Neither is being female easy. Women hear conflicting voices about their role. On the one hand, they are told that traditional roles thwart fulfillment of potential and, on the other hand, they are told that increased employment of women may be linked with increased divorce, more crime and delinquency, and increased alcoholism and schizophrenia among women. Aging is a problem with special difficulties for many women for, psychologically, aging carries a loss of recognition and status for them much more than for the man. Being physically attractive counts for much more in a woman's life than in a man's life. Susan Sontag has pointed out that "femininity" is identified with incompetence, helplessness, passivity, non-competitiveness, and being nice and that age does not improve these qualities. There is also evidence of greater problems related to mental health for women than for men. There are several reasons to assume that women, because of the roles they must fill and the options that may or may not be available, are more likely than men to have emotional problems. There is considerable evidence that women have more negative images of themselves than men and that they are more likely to become depressed than men.

Prayer In Duet

God, we thank you and praise you for creating us as male and female and for teaching us to live and express complementarity and not competitiveness. But, Lord, it's not always easy being a male or a female. Give us the strength to rise above the stereotyped images of what others expect us to think, to feel, and to act and may we always look to your Son who, though he came to earth as male, lived his model life as Ideal Person. Through Him we pray, Amen.

Chapter Eleven

Is "Husbanding" A Fine Art?

Here are some practical suggestions for the men who want to keep the flame of romance burning.

Men, let's talk about the practical aspects of being a husband. As husbands we know we love our wives and respect them. However, there are times in which our demonstrations of love and respect are ineffective or inadequate. I felt that, as a male, it was both presumptuous and inappropriate for me to write this chapter without female assistance; therefore, I turned to Sandra Collins, a respected friend and outstanding student both of the Bible and of family relations, for help in formulating this listing.

1. Communicate with your wife. Do you know what the number one complaint that wives in our society register against husbands? Answer: men's lack of verbal communication with them. As one woman told Charlie Shedd: "You've heard of the Sphinx. I married him." Some of you make only a few guttural sounds to your wives—when you want food, drink, sex, or the channel changed. Several women complain that husbands are non-communicative during and prior to sex relations—a "silent encounter" as though children or parents are sleeping in the same room. I have chuckled over a George Price cartoon from *New Yorker* that has an old couple sitting before a counselor and the woman declaring, "I wouldn't call two Gesundheit's in seven years a sincere effort to communicate."

2. If you love your wife, you ought to say it. Women cannot be told enough that they are loved. When a woman asks if she is loved, she is not asking for information but rather for a deeper sense of security.

3. Remember that affirmation can come through nonverbal communication. If you have trouble expressing your love for your woman verbally, learn to use your hands to transmit the feeling. Touching time is prime time any relationship, for it brings the assurance that "I am worthy enough to be touched." We are not talking about the touches that lead to sex, but the little hugs and squeezes, the arm around the shoulder, the hand that is extended to transmit warmth and give support. An angry mate may say, "Don't come near me—don't touch me!" These words hurt deeply because the power of touch is so great.

4. Offer compliments to your woman, showing that you are excited, exhilirated, and delighted to the point of near delirium to be living with her. Those who study the Hebrew text of Genesis tell us that three times Adam explodes with delight, excitement, and surprise. Shedd suggests that men offer a new compliment each day of the year so that the woman will hear 360 different compliments each year. If you are a spiritual man, you ought to give thanks orally for your wife at the dinner table or during family devotionals.

You could enrich your marriage by looking in on extramarital lovers or at least by considering the dynamics of courtship before marriage. Here is a brief list of things that lovers do that can help your marriage to thrive:

—Lovers generally are very comfortable massaging each other's egos regularly. Affair lovers spend hours telling each other how wonderful, how special, how loving and how understanding the other is. Such words can heal.

—Lovers satisfy the need of each other to be respected. Just as you want to be respected for who you are, and made to feel that what you do and say matters, your mate is no different.

—Lovers take time for closeness. Living in an action-oriented culture, the notion of spending time with your mate just sitting, reading, touching, looking at the sunset—without any other goal in mind—may be perceived as wasted time. But lovers enjoy sharing closeness and warmth.

—Lovers always anticipate needs and desires and move to fulfill them.

—Lovers often create interesting settings and situations. Couples in love go to great lengths to make every moment count. They know the value of keeping their watches synchronized to ensure shared time.

—Lovers rarely try to regulate the behavior of the other.

—Lovers never negate the person they love.

—Lovers show courtesy, politeness, and manners. Lovers say "thank you."

—Lovers communicate their feelings in a variety of manners.

—Lovers take the time and extra effort to add little touches to their relationship. For example, a personal gift usually takes on much more meaning than the actual value of the gift.

—Lovers effortlessly laugh together. The cause of their laughter may be inane, but it is spontaneous and a bridge to more openness and honesty.

5. Continue the courtship all throughout the years of marriage. One good way to maintain courtship is to have at least one day with your wife away from the home and the children each week. Little gifts can be devastatingly effective. Neither the dates nor the gifts need be expensive.

6. Despite what your woman knows and understands, she tends to live on a feeling level. Her feelings are definitely cyclical, somewhat predictable, but extremely difficult to control. Even when she knows there is a biological or chemical reason for her week or so of feeling down (eg. pre-menstrual tension), she has great difficulty getting on top of these feelings. She would appreciate greater sensitivity and more verbal and physical tenderness during that time.

7. Your woman needs affirmation of her femininity, more than of her efficiency, ability to clean house, to cook, or do laundry. There's a needlework picture that says: "I know I'm efficient. Tell me I'm beautiful." "Female" is what she *is;* housework is what she *does.*

8. While your wife is capable of managing the children, the house, and maybe even the bills, she enjoys the feeling that you are a *participant* and not just a roomer. She wants you to participate actively in what is happening in the home, to know what is going on, to take an interest in what essentially makes up her life.

9. There are few visible rewards for housework, cooking, and mothering—no bonuses, no grade reports, no paycheck, no raises, no means of telling where she stands. While your mate may enjoy the work and can take pride in some of it, there is still little sense of accomplishment when the same tasks must be repeated endlessly. It is possible to be busy all day and have little to show for it—to have kept other people's children, to have visited someone ill, to have prepared food for others, to have cleaned closets, to have folded many loads of clothes, to have listened to someone's problems on the phone and to feel at the end of the day that she has accomplished little because the house is not as straight when you come home as it was at 3:00 before the children arrived. She needs to know that someone knows that she is doing something worthwhile.

10. Work to put more fun back into your marriage. Loving people are fun-loving, playful, and often laughing with each other. Doing seemingly foolish but fun things together (either planned or spontaneously) is one way to add vitality to your marriage.

11. Give your wife as much consideration as you would any stranger you might want to impress. Don't take her for granted, believing that she will always be available and responsive to you.

12. Consult your wife on major decisions. Remember you are in partnership.

13. Allow your mate time to be alone. Also encourage her to spend some time with her friends. No matter how much you love her, she needs the stimulation and encouragement from others.

14. Solicit opinions, ideas, and help from your wife on important problems or issues. You and your mate are individuals. If you feed on each other's strengths and offset each other's weaknesses, your

differences can be vital to the personal growth of both of you and can also intensify your marriage. Don't ask for opinions if your mind is already made up.

15. Your woman may feel quite low on your list of priorities even though she knows that she is loved. She may feel that you will give your time to anyone who needs it before you will give it to her. Probably this is because you are sure of her. It might never occur to you to say, "Listen. I can't talk to you now. I need to get home. My wife is expecting me."

16. If you are married to a pious woman, she would appreciate your taking the initiative in prayer or devotional discussions. She may have no doubt that your children know what is important to their father and what he considers valuable and worthwhile, but wish that all of you could have more prayer time and more devotional time as a family.

Peter the apostle said to "be considerate as you live with your wives, and treat them with respect as the weaker partner and as heirs with you of the gracious gift of life" (I Peter 3:7). This means to live with your chosen woman with understanding. Some men spend many thousands to research their business options and markets but expend neither time nor money to assess the needs of their wives. Can you personally answer these questions about your wife?

What does she need?

What makes her happy?

What makes her nervous?

What makes her relaxed?

What makes her depressed?

A Scripture, A Thought, And A Prayer

"Enjoy life with your wife, whom you love, all the days of this meaningless life that God has given you under sun" (Ecclesiastes 9:9).

If I had only . . .
forgotten future greatness
and looked at the green things and the buildings
and reached out to those around me
and smelled the air
and ignored the forms and the self-styled obligations
and heard the rain on the roof
and put my arms around my wife
. . . and it's not too late.

Hugh Prather

Dear God, thank you for the magnanimous gift of your grace and for your second greatest gift to me, my wife. Through Jesus. Amen.

Chapter Twelve

What's Happening With My Man?

For the women we offer a list of more or less predictable developments in the lives of their husbands.

Age is one of the measures we employ to evaluate ourselves. By age we compare our present life against earlier expectations. The human is a thinking and planning animal, observing his social environment, comparing himself/herself with others, and anticipating the future. The statement "I am 40 years old" has far less significance than a statement such as "I am 40 years old and farther ahead than I expected to be at this point in time." In the practical wisdom of our culture certain birthdays are used as crucial guideposts to measure our progress. These birthdays are the 21st (signifying entry into adulthood); the 30th (representing the departure from youth); the 35th (signifying that half of life has been completed); the 40th (meaning the beginning of middle-age); the 50th (the big half-century mark); the 60th (signifying the beginning of old age) and the 65th (signifying the beginning of retirement). The milestones of the aging process remind us that we are finite.

"Life cycle," "life span," and "life course" are terms that have obvious meaning to us. They connote that life is a course, a process, and a journey to be completed. But because the course is not a simple, continuous, unchanging flow, we may speak of the idea of "seasons" in a person's life. We understand the figure of "seasons" as a connection between the seasons of the year and the seasons of the human life cycle. When Frank Sinatra sang the lyrics to "September Song" ("It's a long, long while from May to December/And the days grow short when you reach September") we all knew the lyricist was referring to the contrast between the young and middle adulthood. To speak of the seasons of life is to say that life has a certain shape with a series of stable segments of the total cycle, each having its own distinctive character. Every season is different from the ones that precede it and follow it, however much it may have in common with the other seasons. Each season has its own time; each is important in its own right; each must be understood on its own terms; each is as important as the others.

In recent years great masses of data have been accumulated about specific features of the adult life. The seminal studies of adult life processes have been made by Carl G. Jung, father of the modern study of adult development, Erik Erikson, and Daniel J. Levinson; you may have read Gail Sheehy's *Passages,* the former best-seller which popularized the data and theories of Jung and Eriksen. Using these sources it is possible, then, to provide married women with a listing of the more or less predictable developments in the lives of their husbands. Hopefully the listing here will provide a basis for better understanding of what's going on in the lives of your men. As you read the listing you may find that several of the generalizations about men are also true for women.

20s

1. The span from 17 to 22 is a "zone of overlap", in which the old era is being completed and the new one is starting.
2. Most of the mental and bodily characteristics that have been evolving in the pre-adult years are at or near their peak levels. These remain relatively stable in most cases until around 40.
3. In early 20s, the male forms his first adult self and makes choices establishing initial membership in the adult world. He makes the first major choices, such as marriage, occupation, residence and style of living, that define his place in the adult world. The crucial importance of these decisions combine to produce emotional pressure on the young man. He may be terrified by the conviction that the choices he makes are irrevocable.
4. He is a novice lover, husband, and father. Gradually, often painfully, he grows more understanding and responsible.
5. In the early period, he wants to be "adult" and independent, but feels unprepared for adult life and may seek out a dependent relationship with a protecting-caring-controlling figure other than a parent. Conflict with parents may continue.
6. He needs to test and explore the possibilities for adult living, keep options open, and maximize alternatives, but also feels need to "make something of my life".
7. He may tend to be idealistic and philosophical, silently probing such issues as "Who am I?" "What is truth?" "How do I put my ideals into effect?"

30s

1. A voice within himself says, "If I am to change my life—things to modify, exclude, or add—I must do it now or it will be too late". There is the feeling that time starts to squeeze.

2. Most biological functions remain at their highest levels until 30 and then decline gradually. While there is no male equivalent to the female menapause there are changes in the hormonal levels that have an effect on the physical status and well-being of the man. Early in this decade there is a gradual decline in the secretion of the hormones testosterone and androgen, which affect sexual activity as well as physical strength and loss of hair and teeth.
3. The mid-life transition may begin in late 30s—this is a boundary zone between two great eras in the life cycle.
4. An imminence of settling down is felt along with the need to form a life structure through which his youthful dreams and values can be realized.
5. He may make major decisions about his marriage (reaffirmation, termination, or an affair) and his occupation (reaffirmation or change). While an event may take only a few days or weeks, it is embedded within a process of change that ordinarily extends over a span of several years.
6. This is usually a time of reform, not revolution, but for most men this transition is stressful and a moderate or severe crisis is very common during the 30s. There is a sense of greater responsibilities and pressures as he must give up even more of the little boy within himself.

40s

1. Mental and bodily characteristics begin to decline from earlier peak levels. The sexual drives are decreasing and he may worry about impotence and masculinity.
2. Offspring are in or near adolescence as he passes 40.
3. Relationships change sharply: the nest is emptying and the nuclear family is dividing into separate households. Children now demand less of the father's time and later in this period will likely leave home, creating the need for adjustments in his relationship with his wife and for changes in parental roles.
4. The transition of 40-45 is devoted to the termination of early adulthood and initiation of middle adulthood.
5. There should be less suffering from the tyranny of instinctual drives—lustful passions, capacity for anger and moral indignation, self-assertiveness and ambition.
6. He should be more free from petty vanities, animosities, envies, and moralisms of early adulthood.
7. The quality of love relationships *should* improve (eg. more tenderness, understanding, unselfish).

8. Expect a change in style of work and living, though a man may renew himself toward generativity or may decline to stagnation.
9. He becomes more keenly aware of his own mortality and perhaps his own failure to accomplish early life goals.

The Subsequent Years

1. 55-60 can be a stable period providing a vehicle for completing middle adulthood.
2. In his 60s, he becomes increasingly aware of growing older, although he may not actually believe he is old. Old age is something that happens to others, not to himself.
3. The man who is able to rejuvenate and enrich himself will find his 50s to be a decade of great fulfillment.
4. New family roles of grandparent and father-in-law may develop.
5. The 60s and early 70s *can* be a time of intellectual productivity. The body is more likely to wear out before the mind.
6. The importance of sex roles in the marriage may decline.
7. He must adjust to a loss of status in society since old age generally is not revered.
8. A new era (late, late adulthood) begins about 80. If he makes it to 80, he should expect various infirmities and at least one chronic illness. The process of aging is much more evident than the process of growth. The life structure usually contains only a small territory, a few significant relationshps and a preoccupation with immediate bodily needs and personal comforts. Expect senescence.
9. The male comes to terms with the process of dying, thus making peace with himself in the shadow of death. He may provide others with an example of wisdom and personal nobility.

Two Meditative Thoughts

"Experience is not what happens to a man; it is what a man does with what happens to him" (Aldous Huxley).

"Lord, thou hast been our refuge from generation to generation. . . . All our days go by under the shadow of thy wrath; our years die away like a murmur. Seventy years is the span of our life, eighty if our strength holds; the hurrying years are labour and sorrow, so quickly they pass and are forgotten . . . Teach us to order our days rightly, that we may enter the gate of wisdom" (Psalms 90: 1, 9-10, 12, NEB).

Chapter Thirteen

Is The Mid-Life Crisis Reality or Rationalization?

Here we are looking at the mid-life crisis as the male might experience it, but we will be offering advice to both men and women for coping with this mid-life phenomenon.

The two Chinese characters at the left form the word "crisis." The first character means "danger" and the other "opportunity." These two meanings aptly describe the "mid-life" crisis that commonly afflicts people between the ages of 35 and 55. This period can be dangerous and destructive or it can be an opportunity for renewed growth and productivity.

What do you think of when you hear "mid-life crisis"? A woman hearing the phrase may think of middle-aged husbands, paunchy and balding, settling into a well-polished rut of physical existence, plagued by depression, nervousness, restlessness, indecision and feelings of insecurity and impending doom. Or she may think of some poor husband who tries to look young by "knocking around" the way he sees young people doing, buying a motorcycle or sports car, and taking leave of his family, sometimes via a romantic fling with a much younger woman. You women have seen this happen many times. And you may have asked yourself many times: "Is the male mid-life crisis for real? Is it caused by some real hormonal changes equivalent to a woman's menapause? Or is all of this a rationalization for men to chuck real values they now find boring so that they can rush out and pursue lusty, selfish fantasies?" You may also wonder about what resources the Christian husband may rely on to cope with this phenomenon.

Let's begin with the assumption that the male mid-life crisis is real rather than imaginary. Our concern here is with understanding the mid-life crisis for the mid-life is a time of high risk for marriages. And because a dedicated Christian man's goals and expectations of himself are likely to be much greater than those of a non-Christian, his vulnerability to a crisis of mid-life or to a special anxiety may be greater. We will not take the space required to recite much of the data compiled by psychologists on adult male development, but you might want to consult Jim Conway's *Men in Mid-Life Crisis* (Cook, 1978), a book written from the Christian perspective.

People have surely struggled through the mid-years period for as long as man has been civilized, but there is evidence that these years are now more difficult, at least in advanced societies, than ever before. This is due to technological achievements, medical advancement (such as prolongation of life), the pace of social and cultural change, the challenge to our value system, and the assault on our religious traditions. All of this constitutes a dizzying series of events, thus making it harder than ever for a man to understand his context—to have a sure understanding of what his time on earth means, and what he should try to make it mean—an understanding crucial to surviving mid-life.

The mid-life crisis is not a single event which can be isolated from the rest of a person's life. Its symptoms occur slowly and may not be noticed until they are well developed. Many are simply aggravated or expanded versions of existing behavior patterns or personality traits. It may be impossible to separate the symptoms from their causes. And they may vary widely from individual to individual. We have mentioned already some emotional symptoms. There are some behavioral symptoms as well: inconsistency, reduced leadership ability, retreat from responsibility, a preference for safe decisions, resentment of job and family, radical change in life-style, and heavy drinking. All of these may lead to serious repercussions for the Christian home: infidelity, alcoholism, boredom, frustration, fears, insecurity, and marital discord. All those people who know and love the mid-age man in crisis are also greatly affected by this period of his life.

How does one explain such rapid and dramatic personality and behavioral changes? Just who is prone to the mid-life crisis? What is the major catalyst for such a crisis? Several theories have been offered:

1. Meeting Morality. As the body begins to slow down, as muscles lose their tone and skin sags, as hair either turns gray or falls out, as exhaustion is felt after a round or two of some sport he once could enjoy playing all day, a man at mid-age confronts his own mortality. He may be faced with declining health and the death of his parents. Almost certainly he knows of someone, close friend or associate his age, whose health has taken a sudden turn for the worse and perhaps died. The male thinks of all that he has to do and how little time there is to do it. Dramatic personality changes may be efforts to hide the manifestations of natural aging and/or to take full advantage of the time that is remaining.

2. The Changing Nest. We have noted already that at mid-life there are changes in the structure and activities of a man's family. His wife and children become less dependent on him, less subject to his influence, and less available as sources of recognition, value and ego support. If adolescent children have serious problems, the male feels the heavy weight of parental responsibility. The empty nest phenomenon, long acknowledged as a deep concern of women, is now viewed by many to be of equal importance to middle-aged men.

3. The Goal Gap. By this theory, man's personality is primarily determined by his work and career. At mid-life the male assesses his career achievements in light of earlier aspirations. When he has achieved less than what he aspired to be, he must reconcile himself to this performance gap. In some cases he may feel trapped in his job. The job may seem like a dead-end street. He may wonder if he should revise his goals or lower expectations of himself.

4. Step Aside. The male at mid-life may stand on the sidelines while he observes the more challenging, more arduous, more fulfilling work assignments given to the younger man. The mid-age man feels dispensable, to say the least.

5. Adventure and Wanderlust. For many men in their middle years, the stability and security they have worked for so long and hard in the areas of family, work, and community, are perceived not as safe but rather as stagnating. Home and office routines become ruts. Life lacks challenges and there is little promise of future opportunities for growth and excitement. Thus, the mid-age man strikes out in pursuit of his dream or vision of doing something he has never done before.

Which one of these theories do you think explains the troubled man at mid-life? Well, probably no one theory explains every mid-life crisis; a combination of factors may be at work. And yet there is a common thread that runs through each of these explanations— the assumption that a man's mid-life crisis is caused by threats to his identity. A man's identity consists of those aspects of his personality which have to do with the way in which he defines himself as a person, the way he defines the meaning of his life and the meaning of the lives of others. Each man may plant and root his identity in a different source from other men and thus each faces a different threat (eg. strong family men may be troubled by the "empty nest;" stage performers by vanity insanity; a business manager by "step aside").

When we go to the Scriptures we do not find explicit statements about mid-life crisis. That, of course, is obvious. The Bible does have much to say about anxiety, values, and priorities and it gives us some interesting narriatives. Was David experiencing a mid-life crisis when he lusted after and sent for Bathsheba? Or when he said, "Death stared me in the face—I was frightened and sad" (Psalm 116:3-4)? What about Solomon? Could his pursuit of prolific writing, his interest in wealth and the trappings of power and status, and his contracting of many marriages—could all of this have been an "ego trip" of a frustrated man at mid-life? And how about Elijah? Here is a man who had won a great victory for God and had a great impact for good, but then he had a spiritual and emotional breakdown (cf. I Kings 19). Elijah becomes so depressed that he prefers to die. God was not frustrated at Elijah's self-pity but began to meet his needs— graciously food was provided for the prophet and later Elijah was allowed to take a long journey in which to unwind and think about some deep spiritual questions of meaning. We won't "push" those narratives too far lest someone ask when Methuselah might have experienced a mid-life crisis! But the message from these and many other narratives: God really cares for us and the crisis we experience are opportunities for others to minister to us and for us to grow.

This points us toward another dimension of the mid-life crisis. We may call this dimension spiritual or religious or existential, but it is real. For a man who is facing all the other struggles and temptations of mid-life is likely also to have a spiritual crisis. Conway notes that the male may view God as an enemy, an unfair enemy at that. God the Creator is thus blamed for making him as he is. In effect he says to God: "You made me this way. You gave me these drives and interests. You knew all about the changes that would be coming in my life. You gave me a devoted pair of parents whose strong indoctrination has now caused my conscience to haunt me until I cannot rest. You are the one who allowed temptation to cross my path. You are the one who allowed the human body to age and ultimately die. You are the one ultimately to blame for the mess that I am in." This blaming of God is much the same as the animosity Adam expressed to God in the Garden of Eden ("This woman that YOU gave me, she caused me to sin.").

The ultimate issue may be existential: "Why am I here?" Is the church of any lasting value?" "With that heart attack, God, were you trying to tell me something?" "Where I am going?" "Why must I feel so guilty for indulging myself in some of the pleasures of the world and satisfying some of the appetites you gave me?" These are some of the questions a male may ask. And if a man wants to establish his own autonomy and complete independence, he may assert that there is no God or that the Bible is nothing but a collection of antiquated moral standards. Beyond any question, he is in the greatest turmoil, the greatest struggle, of his life. And most of his solutions to his problems and questions tend to cut off people who could be the most help to him. At a time when the male tries to leave the impression that he has his life all together, he may be trying to camouflage the unravellings at the core of his being.

Thus far you may feel that the mid-life crisis has been at least somewhat described and explained but that there have been no cures offered. But don't go looking for a "cure" because the crisis is not a disease. No medicine or prescription can bring its end. And for that matter, no decisive moment in life can likely reverse it. Only a plan of action implemented with courage can lead to its resolution. Such a plan might involve considering the consequences of any bizarre behavior, resolving any guilt of the past, changing identity so as not to be vulnerable to future threats, formulating realistic expectations of the future and, with the help of significant other(s), integrate these changes into the pattern of his life. Special counseling or psychotherapy may be necessary for the simple reason that pursuing this course of action will lead to some changes that may seem every bit as traumatic as the crisis itself. Courage is always needed to confront a crisis situation.

Some suggestions for middle-aged men:

1. Stop thinking of age and of being a part of a group. You are yourself. Your life had a beginning and it will have an end and you cannot reverse the process, so you might as well accept it. Remember that all age groups and eras have their advantages. So be realistic!
2. Guard your physical health. People who enjoy good health live happier lives than those who do not. Don't avoid annual checkups.
3. Physical exercise seems to clear the mind, drain off some of the emotional tension, and help keep the body in proper tone and shape. You might take up a new sport. Jogging, if you can "hack it," is great for depression and all other negative emotional states.
4. Take a good look at yourself. Assess your strengths, shortcomings, and needs. This will give you a better perspective on yourself. Then consider taking on some new challenges. If one door is closed, then check another one.
5. Exposure to new stimuli is good. Try a change of scenery for vacation time. Traveling is educational and therapeutic. Take some courses or get on a reading program.
6. More clearly define your own personal philosophy. The world continues to undergo tremendous social, cultural, and technological change. The distinction between right and wrong was once relatively

easy, because your immediate society shared your values and you drew strength from that fact. Today, the Christian may have to stand alone and that is difficult, especially if you are not certain or clear about your value system and unable to defend it. What are your values? Forget what everyone else seems to be thinking, or doing, and decide what is right and wrong for *you*. Work on not being overly distressed about those friends and associates who reject your Christian values and convictions—each man reaps as he sows.

7. Make plans for the future, but have a flexible style. If you are 55, assume the Lord just might give you 20 more years. What would you like to accomplish during that time? Would you like to be remembered for some contribution to the world? Do you want to help people? Be creative? Do you have a plan of action? Similarly, how prepared are you to meet the crises you must someday face? Again, a moral value system (a house not built on shifting sand) is of prime importance. Be flexible so that when you face retirement years, you can make the needed adjustments.

8. Seek the help of others. It is not necessary to struggle with the mid-life crisis by yourself. Talk more intimately with your family, but also help may be sought from a close friend, your minister, or a doctor.

9. Keep working on your personality. You don't have to be young forever, but you can continue to be immature. Consider that mental health and emotional stability are *your* business. Neglect neither.

10. Most important, get your spiritual life in order. Establish a right relationship with God. Reorder your priorities so that worship, study, spiritual growth are at the top of the list. Look carefully at what you are giving the Lord and in service to the community of faith and see if you meet your potential. Ask yourself if the projects to which you devote highest energy will have effects which will survive you.

Some suggestions to middle-aged women about their husbands:

Women often appear to be far more concerned than men about the male mid-life crisis and what to do about it. The importance of a helping relationship to the middle-aged man trying to resolve his mid-life crisis cannot be overstated. Most men will look to their existing relationships for the help they need. The "helper" has three major responsibilities: She must

    *Help him to see himself.

    *Help him to understand himself.

    *Help him to change himself.

1. Describe, don't evaluate. This will leave the man free to use the

information or not to use it if he sees fit. If you can avoid evaluative, accusatory language you will reduce the need for him to respond defensively. Statements such as "You should . . . ," or "Why don't you . . .?" or "You'd be better off if . . ." while symbolic of the woman's feeling, are likely to be rejected. (The mirror analogy is important here; a mirror does not judge, but merely reflects.)

2. Be specific, not general. The middle-aged man will be little helped by observations that he seems somehow "different" or "changed." There is little here for the man to act on.

3. Be timely, not random. The timing of communicating such information to the man can be critical. Is he ready to hear it? Can he relate to it now? Where possible, you should wait until the time when he solicits your opinion or at least when he brings the subject up.

4. Try problem-solving, not solution-giving. Few things close a man's eyes and mind quicker than being told, "Here's what you ought to do." A special effort must be made to avoid approaching the man's behavior or personality problems with a view toward teaching him what he should or ought to do, for these imply his inadequacy and are sure to be rejected. Moralizing is never very helpful or appreciated.

5. Offer empathy, not just sympathy. Caring and concern from his point of view without condescension may be the key to helping the man to see himself as clearly as others see him.

6. Help him understand himself. The two of you should explore together the causes of the changes in his life. This can be difficult, because often there are things about you that contribute, even cause, the man's crisis. You might support him if he has any desire to seek additional help. You should not nag him about revealing secrets he has held about past behavior.

7. Help him to change himself and be especially appreciative and supportive of any improvement in spiritual life and experience. Change for any individual is most lasting, has the best chance of becoming part of the individual's personality, when it is rewarded by a significant other person. Actually, you may feel threatened by your husband's effort to change, wondering where all of this motion will lead to. You may wonder if your relationship will change. This might lead to a productive inventory of your own spiritual commitment and life.

Prayer (by Robert Raines from *Lord, Could You Make It a Little Better,* Word, 1972)

Middle-agers are beautiful!
    aren't we, Lord?

I feel for us
    too radical for our parents
    too reactionary for our kids

    supposedly in the prime of life
        like prime rib
        everybody eating off me
          devouring me
        nobody thanking me
          appreciating me

    but still hanging in there
        communicating with my parents
        in touch with my kids

    and getting more in touch
        with myself

    and that's all good

    thanks for making it good,

and

    could you make it a little better?

Chapter Fourteen

How Do I Keep My Man?

Here are some suggestions for the women only.

You women are to be congratulated because you generally take your marriages more seriously and you make a greater emotional investment in them than do your husbands. Also, you are more likely to be the first to seek help when serious marital difficulty arises. Your influence on family life may be greater than you think. Have you thought that you might be the hub of the entire home, that everything might center around you—your attitude, your position with the children, your stance on moral and spiritual matters?

You certainly want your marriage to succeed. Here is a listing of suggestions and insights about men that could serve as a checklist for your interaction with your husband.

1. Since in our culture your husband is a "breadwinner," his career is very important to him. Support him in his work by becoming involved in his work, at least to the extend he would like for you to be involved. This might involve a little special education on your part. You might consider taking a course or reading some books in his field so that you can have at least a minimal understanding of his professional situation and problems and so that you can be a sounding board for his ideas.

2. Nobody, but nobody, must come ahead of your husband. Most women have spent 19-20 years in close relationship with their parents, being totally dependent on them. That heavy dependence might continue after marriage. And, of course, it may be encouraged by parents who consciously want to give their daughters freedom but unconsciously fear to "lose" them. When even middle-age women visit their parents they can be made to feel like little girls again. A husband may feel that his in-laws have more influence with his wife than he does. To add insult to injury, his wife may be critical of *his* parents and family. Never criticize or be rude to his family.

3. Develop a sense of independence. Although you are the weaker vessel, you can be just as strong and capable emotionally and intellectually; and morally, you are just as accountable as the male.

Determine that whatever happens in your marriage, you can survive. Be able to make it on your own. Determine that *nothing* can destroy you (not the death of your husband nor his divorcing you). Communicate this resolution to your husband so he will not take you for granted. You must retain your dignity and self-respect. Nothing douses more water on a romantic flame than for one partner to fling herself emotionally on the other, accepting disrespect in stride. She says in effect, "No matter how you treat me, how unfaithful, how cruelly, I'll still be here at your feet, because I can't survive without you." That is one of the best ways to kill a beautiful friendship.

4. Give praise and appreciation rather than seeking it. Do you think your man needs love, affection, praise, and compliments any less than you do? Both of you need it and you should feel free to take the initiative in giving affection and making love. When there is bad news to share or the day has not been a good one, you might consider communicating this information or feeling at some other time than when your husband walks through the door from work.

5. Be his wife and not his child, thus acting like an adult and treating him like an adult. Surrender possessiveness and jealousy. Your husband may need time to himself. He may need some breathing room. Remember that no man ever loved his wife any more because she was jealous and possessive of him (that may prove her love for him, but there are far better ways to do it) and no man has been made more trustworthy by not being trusted and by being investigated and monitored.

6. Abandon all hope of changing your husband through criticism or attack. Nagging is the major complaint husbands have against their wives. Nagging is the opposite of acceptance and is a self-defeating "method" of changing behavior. "He who harps on something breaks up friendship" (Prov. 17:9 NEB) and "a nagging wife is like water dripping endlessly" (Prov. 19:13 NEB). Wives can make a great issue over "tremendous trifles"—those little habits of husbands that are irritating to them. "A woman who says she can read her husband like a book rarely does," someone has said, "instead of skipping over what she does not like, she goes over and over it."

7. Life can be much more straightforward for men than for women and, in regard to hints and suggestions, men can be obtuse. If you want to get a message across to your man, it may require more than a gentle hint. Do not assume that he is an expert mind-reader.

8. Men are much more sensitive to criticism from women than women may realize. Be gentle with him—especially in public. And comparing him with other men (either favorably or unfavorably)

could make him uncomfortable. Praise is always welcome, but not always on a comparative basis.

9. Do not criticize your husband for having a hobby. Love for his hobby does not mean that he loves you or your children any less. His hobby may be a necessary ingredient to mental health; he does it to relax totally and find relief from the pressures of work and the world. If you want a happy husband, don't make him feel guilty over a reasonable amount of time with his hobby.

10. If you want him to get better at little romantic remembrances, then praise him for the least little one, even if he did it almost by accident. He enjoys being successful at wooing his woman and will "fall all over himself" trying to repeat his "success." Be careful not to reject his gentle romantic overture; such rejection could be worse to him than a setback at work.

11. Work and love of work compete with home and love of your family. Both are required for a stable and emotionally healthy manhood. Men are keenly aware of this competition for time and attention between work and family life. Most men wrestle with this dilemma through much of their careers. A good man's heart is big enough to love work, wife, and family. However, he needs your understanding and gentle prodding to keep them balanced properly.

12. Give thanks to God for a good husband. Sure, you do not have a perfect husband, but what woman does? You accepted his proposition to share his life, his support, and wear his name, so be grateful for his good qualities. In treating him like an adult, do not take him (his love, his courtesies, his gifts) for granted. If you have a husband who is a good provider, works hard, is honest, has good habits, treats you with love and tenderness, puts you first—then praise the Lord and give thanks for him. Whatever else he may be, remember that he chose you. And every time he comes home, he chooses to come home. And if he is a man who goes to great effort to be a spiritual leader in the home, if he prays at your meal time, he relates discussion and problem-solving to Biblical truth, if he reads the Bible, attends worship with you; encourages you to do what is right; loves your children—then be especially grateful, for such husbands are rare.

Poem And Prayer

Someone asked me
To name the time
Our friendship stopped
And love began.

Oh, my darling,
That's the secret
Our friendship
Never stopped.
Lois Wyse

Dear God, thank you for the magnanimous gift of your grace and for your second greatest gift to me, my husband. Through Jesus. Amen.

Chapter Fifteen

How Do We Improve Our Communication?

Since any relationship is only as good as its communication and since no human relationship is any more important than marriage, we need constantly to work at making our communication system effective.

"We just don't communicate" is a common complaint of husbands and wives. But marital communication is inevitable despite many feelings to the contrary. You can turn off the television or radio. You can avoid books, newspapers, and magazines. You can boycott the theatre. But as long as you live in a household with another human being, you will communicate—if not verbally, then with gestures or even with periods of silence. "We just don't communicate" is better translated as "I don't like what we communicate," or "I don't like the way we communicate," or it may also mean "We just don't trust each other enough to reveal our true feelings about anything."

Do you know how important good communication is to your marriage? Communication is to marriage what blood is to the body. "If there is any one indispensable insight with which a young couple should begin their life together," says Reuel Howe, "it is that they should try to keep open, at all cost, the lines of communication between them." The happiness and fulfillment of you and your mate's marriage may be measured in terms of the deepening dialogue which characterizes your union.

Misconceptions About Communication

Several myths and misconceptions make communication, even between intimates, a delicate and difficult process:

—There is the assumption that after years of marriage mates can read each other's minds. Of course in many cases mates can know exactly what is being thought and felt by the other. You should know your mate better than anyone else in the world. And yet, people and situations are always changing and you cannot assume that you and your partner have an adequate understanding on matters that you have not discussed. To assume understanding is to court misunderstanding.

—There is the assumption that communication is simply the transfer of meaning from one mind to another. To transfer something suggests moving material objects from one place to another. Ideas and feelings are not "transferred" in this way. Some filtering and distortion of the ideas and feelings communicated is inevitable. Communication is a process involving the sorting, selecting, and sending of symbols through voice, language, and body in order to enable the receiver to perceive and recreate in his/her own mind the meaning intended. Symbolic behavior is always subject to variant interpretation. As a matter of fact, most speakers send more than one message at the same time, a major reason for inaccurate communication.

—There is the assumption that meaning is in words or messages. In a sense, words do not mean anything and dictionaries do not and cannot provide us with meanings. Meanings are in people as personal property. You are free to learn meanings, add to them, distort them, forget them, change them. To the extent that you and another person have similar meanings (based on similar experiences and shared values) you can communicate. Serious breakdowns in communication can be attributed to the false assumption that there is meaning in the message, rather than only in the source and receiver.

—There is the assumption that the significant people in our lives all share the same world view and same understanding about values and human behavior.

—The greatest misconception of all is that communication is an easy and simple process. Nothing could be further from the truth! Communication is learned behavior that involves the mastery of skills. The great surprise is not that people fail to communicate, but that they actually communicate on important occasions even though they give little thought to developing communications skills.

Despite the problems you may encounter at different times, there are ways the two of you may improve your communication. Simply being aware of how you communicate is an important method of improving your skills. Several good books on communication are available for your study. When you develop communication skills you enhance your ability to become intimate.

Communication And The Authentic Self

When we talk about improving our communication, we are not

concerned simply with better ways to say "Looks like rain, doesn't it?" or "Pass the salt." Such cliche-ridden and superficial talk is little more than social gesture. It is through communication that you reveal yourself to others. Mutual self-revelation is the basis for intimacy. You know that much of your life is spent in roles—as husband, wife, son, daughter, father, mother, club member, worker, student—and you usually act and live these roles conventionally. These roles do not necessarily reflect your deeper self and reveal to others who you really are and what you are all about. You can get to the point where even you do not know who you are. Through the process of revealing yourself to others you discover who you are. In the process of sharing, another shares with you. Self-disclosure is reciprocal.

You undoubtedly want to be authentic personal being, to have integrity and sincerity. That instinctive dimension of the human spirit must surely be part of the divine nature that the Creator has imparted to you. You know that truly worthwhile relationships are built on those qualities of authenticity of self, integrity, and sincerity; you know also that relationships are destroyed by hypocrisy, sham, and pretense. But because of the roles you must assume and because self-disclosure can be disadvantageous, it can be difficult to be truly yourself. Ideally, it is in your marriage that you can dedicate yourself to full self-disclosure; apart from such commitment, marriage does not achieve its highest potential for fulfillment.

The more that you "play games" or wear masks at home and the more efforts at little or large deception that you make, the more the foundation of intimate relationship is eroded. If you do not disclose yourself, you receive no feedback from your partner. You do not know yourself better nor does your partner know himself/herself better. You then remain in a closed relationship, isolated and untouched by the other. If you do not disclose yourself, neither will your mate. Your silence obliges him/her to remain silent. If you do not disclose yourself, you will remain ignorant of yourself because your mate will not speak to you candidly. Your mate will tell you only what he/she believes you want to hear because you are afraid to reveal yourself.

Have you ever thought of Jesus as the ultimate communication model? Certainly you have thought of Jesus being completely honest and sincere, but have you thought of how this meant Jesus could be free, open, spontaneous, natural, and uninhibitied, with all kinds of people. Jesus abhorred all falseness, concealment, and pretense; he reserved his most scathing rebukes for hypocrites, those whose manner and words left the impression of pious devotion but whose hearts and lives were far from God. Jesus always spoke the truth in love, was fully approachable and was never reluctant to answer a sincere questioner. He was willing to be fully known and in revealing himself, he revealed God. We all can learn from this perfect model.

Ask yourself: "Am I honestly willing and able to tell others who I am?" If you can honestly tell your partner who you are—ie., what you think, judge, feel, esteem, value, prefer, love, hope for, hate, fear, dread, believe in, and are committed to (as well as what you doubt, disbelieve, and are not committed to)—then you have the basis for an intimate marriage and you have laid the foundation for reaching your full potential as a person. Such honesty means that your exterior accurately reflects your interior. It means that in the drama of your life your front-stage behavior synchronizes with your backstage behavior. (Front-stage behavior takes place publicly among non-intimates, while backstage behavior takes place privately among intimates. Marital and family behavior can be either. Keeping certain kinds of behavior backstage makes privacy easier to achieve, but it also makes it difficult to compare our own experiences with those of other people and leads us to be unrealistic in our expectations of ourselves and others.)

Other questions: Do you feel you are as open and honest with your mate as you could be? Are there areas of your thinking that you exclude from everyone? Do you think it is possible in a marriage that several things be left unsaid? Are you more honest with another in certain areas than you are with your mate? Do you create an atmosphere where your mate is free to communicate his/her thoughts, fears, and to discuss his/her values, to expose his/her fears and frustrations, to admit his/her failures and shames and share his/her triumphs? Are you truly transparent to each other?

These questions get at the heart of a successful and fulfilling marriage. Perhaps teenagers and the very newly wed believe that good sex is the key to great marriage. But good sex, vital as it is as a form of non-verbal communication, has never yet by itself settled a real difference between partners or preserved a marriage that was not working effectively at other significant levels of interaction. It is spoken language, all that talk between you and your partner, that must serve as the primary means of your coming to know each other in depth.

Please keep in mind that the kind of depth communication that involves mutual self-disclosure, a knowing and being known, demands sufficient time to occur. This kind of intimacy does not happen overnight. God spent hundreds of years fully revealing himself through the pages of Biblical history. Surely you would expect it to take you at least a lifetime to make yourselves known to each other in marriage.

Seven Guidelines That Will Help Your Relationship Flourish

1. Cultivate the habit of delivering "I" messages than "you" messages.

Here are two simple messages: "Why do you keep putting so much salt in this dish?" and "I'd prefer less salt in the casserole." Or again: "You think you know so much about everything, don't you?" and "I resent hearing answers, especially when I don't think there's a question." The first statements are "you" messages that project the burden of the idea onto the other person, making the other defensive and possibly evoking an angry and aggressive reply. But the other messages are "I" messages; the speaker is owning up to the responsibility for the ideas. "I" language is responsible, honest, direct, immediate and it risks taking a position. "You" language focuses on the other in blaming, accusing, analyzing, diagnosing, prescribing, and trying to change the other. Every time you feel a "you" message coming on, head it off.

2. Always respond to what your partner has said.

Most of us respond in some way to messages from our mates, but we do not always respond to the issue raised in the message. Suppose a woman comes in from grocery shopping at the end of the day and her husband asks "Did you pick up the license plates today?" and the woman replies, "What? Do I have to do all the family errands around here? Maybe you could do something for all of us occasionally. After all, you do most of the driving!" With that exchange the communication bloodletting has begun. The wife should have completed the transaction by saying, "No, I forgot to get the license plates," and then later have raised the new issue of her feeling of having to do the bulk of the work in the family.

3. Give your mate complete freedom of speech and feeling.

You can turn your mate into a deaf mute by evaluating and judging him/her and everything that is said. A harsh, judgmental statement is a "take-away," because it takes away the legitimacy and validity of the other person's feelings (for example, "How could you do such a thing?" or "How could you be so gullible as to believe such a thing?"). The "take-away" is a lethal mixture of cynicism and incredulity. It is certain to cut off your mate's desire to share feelings.

On the other hand, four of the most loving words that can be spoken in any relationship are: "Tell me about it."

4. Set aside talking time just for the two of you.

You have to be on guard always lest the busyness of your lives all but eliminate times for sharing. Several studies measuring the amount of time that couples spend in verbal exchanges with each other have been conducted and the findings are startling. Some couples may spend as little as five minutes per day talking with each other. How is it in your marriage? Suppose there was a voice-activated tape recorder which recorded only the spoken exchanges between you and your mate during the day and that you were to replay the tape at the end of the day—how long would the tape play? So often what we have to communicate never gets beyond the trivia of the day. Of course anything may be a topic for conversation, but what you *do* is never quite as important as what you *are* or hope *to be*.

5. Don't label your mate or yourself and avoid sweeping generalizations.

Modern society seems to need labels. From cans to cars to candidates, enormous sums of time and money are spend categorizing everything. Labels are intended to be a shorthand method of identification and as such are necessary. But when they are used for people, labels can have long-lasting, detrimental effects. Have you ever been forced to live *up* to or live *down* a label, such as "black sheep," "mama's boy," or "daddy's girl"? Labeling can have a disastrous effect on intimacy. When you label yourself, you bind yourself to the past, thus inhibiting personal growth. You label your mate because it makes him/her easier to deal with—static, unchanging and, thus, easier to get a handle on. But this really is an illusion, because you are not seeing the real person, just a shadow of your mate. When you catch yourself saying to your partner "You always . . ." or "You never . . ." then you are guilty of labeling, even when the remark is intended to be complimentary.

6. Develop a sense of timing

There is a rhythm to living together just as real as sunrise and sunset. There is a time to talk, a time to listen, and a time to leave your partner alone. Success or failure in communication may often depend on whether we know these times. Trying to argue an issue is pointless when one mate is exhausted from the day's work. A request for sexual intimacy is poorly timed when previous glances and overtures only provoked irritation. Small talk about trivialities is not needed when one is depressed.

7. Learn to listen all over.

Listening is strenuous activity. When you listen with your body, mind, and spirit, it is what Theodore Reik calls "listening with your third ear." Active listening consumes time and energy but is less exhausting than failures in understanding. Listening is so important that we'll have more to say about it in the next chapter.

Thought For Mediation

For communication to have meaning
it must have a life.
It must transcend "you and me" and become "us."
If I truly communicate, I see in you
a life that is not me and partake of it.
And you see and partake of me.
In a small way we then grow out of our old selves
and become something new.
To have this kind of sharing
I cannot enter a conversation clutching myself.
I must enter it with loose boundaries.
I must give myself to the relationship,
and be willing to be what grows out of it.

Hugh Prather

Chapter Sixteen

Are You Really Listening?

An intimate relationship is only as good as its communication and since half or more of effective communication is listening we need to give careful attention to developing listening skills.

It begins innocently enough. A man arrives home late from work on a busy Monday. His wife has many important things to share with him about the beginning of her busy week so she allows him the privilege of enjoying his supper without discussing the matters that concern her most. But after supper the man retires to his favorite recliner and turns on the television because it is time for "Monday Night Football." For the next three hours there is no shortage of words being uttered in the house. Only thing, most of the words come from Frank Gifford, Don Meredith, or the garrulous Howard Cosell. Oh yes, the wife does attempt to talk to her husband but he is hardly tuned in to her. The half-time break and commercial slots are spent with the husband faking attention to his wife all the while perusing the newspaper. And before long, without even realizing how it came about, a deadly silence grows between them.

The fact is, listening, like a marriage, is a partnership. It is a shared responsibility between the person speaking and the person listening. And if the listener doesn't show genuine interest and sensitivity to what's being said, the speaker will stop talking. And the communication effort will fail. The result? The marriage relationship deteriorates. Feelings are not shared, at least at home. New ideas are stillborn. Agenda is left unattended. Growth stops. The presence of love is questioned, maybe doubted.

Deep within you and all other humans is a profound need to be heard and understood, understood not in part but as a whole. When only a part of you is understood, that part which is unrecognized and unknown presses hard for attention. Little wonder, then, that the failure to listen is a chief complaint that spouses level against each other. "You weren't even listening to me!"—have you ever heard that complaint made around your house? Perhaps you were only half listening, assuming that you knew the other half of the story. Or perhaps you were not sufficiently impressed with the significance of the subject matter so that your mind found more delight in other preoccupations or even in fantasy. Or perhaps there were too many other matters on your mind that demanded silent attention. The reasons for non-attentiveness are many.

The essence of love, as you know, is giving. And we give ourselves by listening. The process of falling in love is a process of giving almost obsessive attention to the words, manner, wishes, and needs of the cherished person. Communication between two intense lovers is almost the only thing that really matters to them. After years of married life, your listening habits are likely to undergo some change. Have you ever wondered if there was some other man/woman in your partner's life? Well, if there were, that other person is not difficult to identify. Dwight Small points out that "the other woman" is the one listening attentively to an emotionally deprived husband. She may not be younger, prettier, sexier, or smarter than this wife; she may fall short of his wife in many areas and does not know him as well as his wife. Yet she is eager to listen to whatever presently interests or concerns him and is slow to pass judgment on what he thinks, feels, or says. This he finds exciting and comforting; he feels appreciated and understood.

When you listen as an act of loving and caring, it is a healing process. The exact nature of this process will forever remain a mystery, but whenever you have received the blessing of another's listening you may feel that God's grace has been mediated in some way in your life. When someone listens to your deepest hurts and most difficult anxieties, you feel that you have been fully accepted for who you are.

Jesus is our model for listening. You may have heard the remark, "Jesus spent thirty years listening and three years speaking." Hardly accurate, of course, but the point is clear. As you read the gospel narratives surely you are impressed by the times Jesus shared the Father's love by being available to listen. Not only did he listen to Nicodemus, to the unnamed Samaritan woman at the well, to Zaccheus, to his disciples, but he listened always to his Father's voice. The one who knew all things and had so much to communicate and so little time to speak was the very one who spend much time in listening. Remember that in interpersonal dialogue it is as much or more great listening that makes for great speaking as it is great speaking that makes for great listening.

Seven Suggestions For Effective
Listening In Marriage

1. Make a firm initial commitment to listen.

Listening is hard work. It requires energy. Decide you are going to listen better now than you have in the past.

2. Get physically and mentally ready to listen.

Check your posture. Turn off (or at least turn down) the television or radio. Put away the paper or book you were reading unless you plan to use it. Try to dismiss personal worries, concerns, or pleasant reverie until a decision to discuss them later.

3. Give your partner a full hearing.

Avoid interrupting your mate unless you are certain you understand the message fully and that such interruption is necessary. Impatience with a speaker can lead to false understanding or agreement and may eventually lead to greater difficulty.

4. Listen with all of your body.

Effective listening means becoming aware of all the cues that your mate emits and this implies an openness to the totality of communication. You do not listen just with your ears. You listen with your eyes and with your sense of touch and you "listen" to your own feelings and emotions that arise in you because of the contact with your mate. You listen to your mate's words, of course, but you must be tuned in to the messages encoded in the cues that surround the words (the "metacommunications" of your mate)—the voice, the demeanor, the vocabulary, the gestures, the context, the linquistic patterns, and the bodily movements. You also listen to the "sounds of silence." The "good vibes" and "bad vibes" most people notice in their communication are probably responses to nonverbal cues.

5. Eliminate obstacles to effective listening.

A number of things can get between you and your mate in the listening process:

Self-consciousness: becoming preoccupied with yourself so that you do not hear what your mate is saying.

—Dreaming: getting lost in your own reveries so that you are thinking only of what was said to you 15 minutes ago or even earlier in the day.

—Interrupting: injecting your own views before your mate has finished speaking. Such interruption is a personal affront and is handled defensively.

—Excessive talking: chattering ceaselessly and aimlessly to avoid what the mate wants to say or warding off his/her disturbing message.

—Hearing what you want to hear: this needs no comment.

—Reductive listening: modifying a new message so that it sounds like previous messages. This is a refusal to admit that your mate or situations can change.

—Message anxiety: distorting the message because of fear, bias, or prejudice. When a message is suffused with emotion, it is likely to arouse the anxiety of both the speaker and the listener. There is no simple solution to this problem, but watch out! Message distortion is right around the corner.

Undoubtedly you can think of some other obstacles to effective listening.

6. Listen empathically.

Accurate empathy is absolutely essential to growthful interpersonal relations. It requires you to get inside your partner, to view the world through his/her eyes, and to communicate to your partner your understanding of him/her. In empathy you think the thought and feel the feeling of the other. You see, you feel, you understand, and you respond as if you were, in fact, the other person. Empathy means you will suspend judgment and understand what your mate means in terms of his/her frame of reference before you react.

7. Pay attention to feedback and give feedback.

Empathy is facilitated by feedback. Feedback employs such questions as, "Do I hear you to say . . . ?" or "What you are telling me is . . ." "The next time you get into an argument with your wife," Carl Rogers tells the men, "just stop the discussion for a moment and for an experiment, institute this rule. 'Each person can speak up for himself only after he has first restated the ideas and feelings of the previous speaker accurately, and to that speaker's satisfaction.' . . . Once you have been able to see the other's point of view, your own comments will have to be drastically revised. You will also find the emotion going out of the discussion, the differences being reduced, and those differences which remain being of a rational and understandable sort."

Scriptures

"Do not judge, or you too will be judged" (Matt. 7:1).

"Consider carefully how you listen" (Luke 8:18).

"My dear brothers, take note of this: Everyone should be quick to listen, slow to speak and slow to become angry, for man's anger does not bring about the righteous life that God desires. . . .

(James 1:19-20)

Chapter Seventeen

Does Severe Conflict Mean That We Do Not Have A Christian Marriage?

Even for Christians anger and conflict are natural dimensions of intimacy and when managed creatively they do much more to enhance the quality of a marriage than does a phony "peace" which denies reality.

You've seen those pictures on the covers of Christian magazines and Sunday School literature—those slick, color photographs that depict a smiling, well-scrubbed, immaculately dressed, perfectly-groomed couple sitting around the house just enjoying some leisure activity of their children. For this couple, faith issues in perfect peace, undisturbed by any harsh words. The concluding line from many a fairy tale—"And so they were married, and lived happily ever after"—seems fairly appropriate for such a couple.

The first conflict within your marriage may have come as a shock to you. You started out "in love," expecting your home to be, if not a castle, at least a retreat from the jungle outside. And then you may have found the reality to be quite different. You realized you could have disagreements outside the home, at work as well as with the many people you encounter in daily life (clerks, traffic patrolmen, office mates, parking lot attendants, tennis opponents, etc.), but you may have found these disagreements to be minor compared with the conflict, the angry outbursts that *can* happen at home—that is, unless you learned all of this before you got married.

The problem is that many good people are victimized by Christian stereotypes, such as the one fostered by pictures in Christian publications of married couples. You may smile inside when you hear someone say to friends "Oh, my mate and I never disagree," for you know that disagreement is inevitable in a marriage. But you may feel that anger is incompatible with Christian faith and that any serious conflict between persons should be understood as a manifestation of sin and brokenness. If you feel that anger and conflict are wrong, intimacy with you mate may deteriorate through poor communication, suppression, and even dishonesty.

Here are some important factors about marital conflict to realize:

(1) Conflict is a natural part of intimacy. A relationship which spells closeness also spells conflict. And that is the paradox of love—the more intimate you become, the more likely there are to be differences. Conflict between people who love each other seems to be a mystery. You expect love to unify lovers, but it doesn't always. The co-existence of love and conflict has been an enigma to human beings for centuries. An ancient Sanskrit poem asks why:

> In the old days we both agreed
> That I was you and you were me.
> But now what has happened
> That makes you, you
> And me, me?

(2) As painful as conflict is, it performs several important functions. In a relationship, conflict is a way of maintaining personal boundaries. It is a way of acknowledging the values, needs, interests, and concerns of the other person. The strength of your marriage, or any other social organization for that matter, comes from the continued existence of the individual elements. The United States provides a good analogy. The nation is one and sovereign with federal rule supreme, but the 50 states maintain their own identities and by their uniqueness contribute to the overall richness and vigor of the union. And conflict is a way of sharpening communication skills, since it often originates from poor communication.

Most important, conflict can lead to change. For many people, the status quo, no matter how unsatisfactory and unpleasant, is less threatening than an uncertain and untried family arrangement. Little wonder, then, that couples frequently avoid conflict by covering up their differences. Unfortunately, however, repressing feelings, desires, and needs does not make these psychological elements disappear. The consequence may be a gradual but deadly alienation or an explosive buildup of anger. And frequently the conflict has merely been postponed to a time when it is much harder to deal with. The prophets of God rendered harsh judgment on those who pretended everything was all right rather than face honestly the faults in themselves and in their society. The false prophet is one who says "Peace, peace, when there is no peace" (cf. Jere. 6:14; 8:11; Ezek. 13:10-11, 14-16).

(3) Being one may only be an illusion for many married couples. Two people do not become one just because they develop some love for each other. Their love may not be an illusion, but their sense of ultimate oneness is. The two retain their individual identities, needs, wants, and a lot of excess baggage from past relationships.

In every marriage, Dwight Small points out, there is the existence of two opposing principles: completion and competition. Completion is imperfect at best while conflict from competition is continually created at deep levels. One comes to marriage with deep love for another only later to discover he loves himself more than the other. Conflict arises from the needs of self-devotion and the needs of devotion to the other. Two values can be at cross purposes. It is a rude shock to many that one cannot relinquish an independent, self-devoted and self-directed life merely by taking a marriage vow. There may be two strong wills in a power clash. The trouble with most quarrels is the mate's attempt to remake or remodel the other.

(4) Anger can be a part of any marriage. And why shouldn't it be? As David Mace points out, the state of being married probably generates more anger in the average man or woman than does any other social situation in which he/she is habitually involved. While it may seem blasphemous to portray marriage in these terms, the media attention in recent years to battered children, battered wives, and even a few battered husbands has lifted a veil that has discreetly concealed what is really going on in many "respectable" families. Suppression of anger is thought to be a positive virtue. Most of the trouble experienced with conflict management arises from the fact that couples do not know how to deal with anger. Yet dealing with anger may be the critical issue affecting the success or failure of the relationship of the great majority of Christian couples.

(5) Conflict, almost by definition, is a painful experience; the word literally means "to strike together." But conflict does not threaten intimate relationships. It is how conflicts are resolved that determines whether relationships are threatened. Conflict that is properly managed can strengthen understanding, deepen intimacy, and help you to know who you really are. If conflict sometimes feels like a painful death in your relationship, its resolution can lead to new life, a relationship of a renewed and richer nature. According to management theory, there are five specific methods of dealing with conflict:

(a) *Competing* is assertive and uncooperative—an individual pursues his own concerns at the other person's expense. This mode is power-oriented and is strongly defensive.

(b) *Accommodating* is unassertive and cooperative—the opposite of competing. Here, the individual neglects his own concerns to satisfy the concerns of the other person.

(c) *Avoiding* is unassertive and uncooperative—the individual does not pursue his own concerns or those of the other person; he does not address the conflict. He withdraws from a threatening situation.

(d) *Collaborating* is both assertive and cooperative—the opposite of avoiding. An effort is made to fully satisfy the concerns of both.

(e) *Compromising* is intermediate in both assertiveness and cooperativeness, the goal of which is to find some middle ground of mutually acceptable solution that satisfies both parties. Compromising gives up more than competing but less than accommodating. It addresses issues directly.

What are the sources of marital conflict? You know that husbands and wives fight about virtually everything and anything—which car to buy, how to spend money, where to spend a vacation, how to discipline children, which television program to watch, whether to entertain friends, who ate the last piece of cake, who messed up the den, who tracked in mud. Marriage counselors and sociologists will tell you that most marital conflict involves sex, money management, or in-laws. Yet, for all this variety, most fights can be placed under one of three major categories:

(a) *Situation conflicts* are probably the most common; they rise out of everyday life and are often totally unexpected. You want to eat out and your mate does not; you are willing for your daughter to have a date and your partner is not; you want to attend a church social and your partner does not; you are willing for your son to drive the family car alone and your partner is not. A simple misunderstanding may be a frequent starting point for a situational conflict. Usually, situational conflicts are short-lived and when they are recollected they seem silly or outrageous.

(b) *Personality conflicts* are more serious and deeper-rooted than situational conflicts. Familiarity may or may not breed contempt, but it certainly does magnify the differences between people. You have found it relatively easy to overlook the habits, beliefs, and quirks of the peripheral people in your life, but you know it is almost impossible to dismiss even the most subtle ways of the one you live with, not to mention larger issues such as temperament and values. People tend to get on each other's nerves. You would expect conflict in obviously "unequally yoked" marriages—say, a nondrinker married to an alcoholic or a devout person married to an atheist. In most marriages, however, the conflict focuses on lesser matters; for example, when one smokes and the other does not there is dispute over scattered ashes and house odor. And, of course, there are ongoing disputes, such as over caps left off toothpaste tubes, dirty clothes on the floor, beds unmade, books and magazines strewn over the house, amount of sugar in the tea, length of time in the bathroom, amount of water used for bathing. Since habits are well ingrained after a few years, personality conflicts can become intense.

(c) *Structural conflict* relates to the wielding of power, or who calls the shots, in your family. This kind of conflict can be deadly. We have already discussed authority relationships in marriage in chapter 8. Authority is based in law but power is based in personality. Suffice it to say here, to the extent that power is the prevailing force in a relationship—whether between you and your mate, between you and your children, or between you and your colleagues—to that extent love and intimacy are diminished.

In the next chapter we will get practical and list some ground rules for the resolution of your marital conflict.

Prayer

"O God, give us serenity to accept what cannot be changed, courage to change what should be changed, and wisdom to distinguish the one from the other."

(A familiar prayer attributed to Reinhold Niebuhr)

Chapter Eighteen

How Should Our Conflict Be Resolved?

Christian mates are as justified in quarreling and fighting as anyone else, but the ground rules should be clear.

I recall counseling with a middle-aged couple, both of whom were members of the congregation I served as pulpit minister. There was a great deal of hostility in their feelings toward each other but I had hoped that several sessions of seeing them, both together and individually, had helped them quarrel cnstructively. After I moved to another city I learned that this couple had obtained a divorce; but apparently their fighting did not end with the divorce. A friend sent me a little newsclip from the local paper which said: "Charged with assault by spitting in the face of Jo Ellen _______, Jim _______ was fined $25 and costs." You might imagine that I marked this up as one couple that I knew I had failed to help with conflict resolution.

Whatever the cause of a family conflict, and however much one of you might be gaining from it, there comes a time when all parties wish to see the issue settled. If the conflict is not ended you will move to a state of virtual emotional divorce which characterizes too many marriages already. Most people in conflict will long for new periods of agreement and stability. How the transition is made between conflict and peace is often more important than what issues the conflict was all about.

Arguing is certainly not the answer. At best, arguing is a kind of sand-lot debate in which both partners hope to find the truth so that the conflict will disappear. But marital arguments often get out of hand because of the emotional subject matter; it's not like you're debating the relative merits of wage and price controls. Arguments also get out of control because they are usually not refereed. The argument turns into a war of words. Is there not a better way to resolve conflict? Aren't words necessary in any conflict resolution?

Conflicts can be resolved by fair fighting. You may think that "fighting" is not an appropriate term for Christian mates who want to resolve their differences fairly. Perhaps fighting connotes physical violence and God only knows how many Christian mates have been physically abused. But we will use the term in the sense that it is employed by psychologist and marriage counselor George Bach. Bach's counseling technique is called "fight training," a method in which couples learn the value and skills of clean, aggressive verbal fighting. "With real intimates," Bach notes, "the start of a fight is a signal that there ought to be some changes made and they know that if the fight is fought properly, chances are that it will clear the air and hopefully result in improvements for both."

The following is not a lengthy and detailed discussion of methods of conflict resolution. Such a discussion may be found in *The Intimate Enemy: How to Fight Fair in Love and Marriage* by George Bach and Peter Wyden (Avon, 1968). Here I am offering ten rules for Christian couples to follow in having a good, clean fight and resolving conflict.

1. Recognize That Differences Do Exist. Be Aware Of The Problem And Then Define It.

It is important to know what you are fighting about. Awareness of a problem usually starts with an awareness of the symptoms. Sometimes a person will do something drastic to get a mate's attention. A man I know who has been unhappily married for many years has gone to a lawyer several times and had divorce papers served on his wife only to withdraw from the proceedings just before the court date; apparently he is unable or unwilling to find another method of communicating his dissatisfaction to his wife. A problem may develop only gradually. Either way, the problem must be defined, common ground of agreement must be established, origin of the problem should be located, and factors in its evolving to the present should be pinpointed. Questions must be raised: Whose needs are not being met? Whose views are being ignored? Some couples cannot handle these issues successfully without a family therapist.

2. Choose The Time And Place For Fighting By Mutual Consent.

The author of Ecclesiastes says that there is "a time to be silent and a time to speak . . . a time for war and a time for peace" (3:7-8); that certainly is true of marital disagreements. Fighting by appointment may seem like a rather ridiculous idea to you, but it has several advantages. Both of you have time to think before you get to the meetings, so all of those things you wish to say can be made clear at the right time—not in private post-mortems. Furthermore, words tend to be less colored by emotion and more by reason if a brief delay occurs between the thought and the expression.

While it is best not to argue when you are excited, angry, or tired, you can allow too much time to pass after the agony of a strong negative emotion. So engage your partner as soon as possible after the issue presents itself. Some fights are alcohol-contaminated, thus making the fighting potentially more bitter and divisive. And there are times not to broach certain subjects; your partner may put out signals that say, "Do not disturb—Refueling."

3. Always Give Your Mate A Chance To Express Himself/ Herself.

There is great value in verbalization. When feelings are expressed they tend to have lost their intensity. When feelings are bottled up or denied expression they become more intense. Anger, for example, is part of the human personality, like the sex drive. It can be displaced, channeled, modified, or repressed—but it cannot go away. This is why efforts should be designed to make people face negative emotions and decontaminate them as sensibly as human fallibility permits.

4. Make Every Effort To Understand The Feeling And Thinking Of Your Mate And To Understand How Your Behavior Affects Your Mate.

This is empathy, of course. We have already stated that empathy is the secret of good communication. If your mate feels that you are making an honest effort to understand his/her point of view, much progress can be made toward the resolution of your problem.

You might ask yourself how you would feel if someone criticizes you, misunderstands you, ridicules you, ignores you. This kind of questioning can help you avoid dirty tricks in conflict resolution. You need also to be aware of how the tensions of the day affect the way you fight your intimate. The man who says something humiliating or demeaning to his wife may merely be reflecting something in his day's work which he has suffered without the opportunity to "work through" or retaliate. The etiquette of public relations and job security has dictated that he keep his feelings bottled up. Then he may unload his frustrations on his wife or his children at the slightest provocation. Such ventilation is hostile scapegoating.

Your all-too-human tendency is to get irritated with others in direct proportion to your irritation with yourself. Sometimes you may even refuse to acknowledge your own errors and instead you project them onto others with whom you intimately associate. The failure to take full personal responsibility for your emotions is a common communication block.

5. Fight Fairly And Cleanly, Avoiding Dirty Tactics And Tricks.

There are many ways to fight dirty. One common way is to dredge up the past, using yesterday's failures as today's ammunition. While men accuse women of this, both sexes seem equally capable of perpetrating this dirty trick. Many people nurse grudges about past mistreatment and they rival the IBM computer in being able to catalogue, isolate, store, and retrieve negative information with the greatest of ease. This tactic has been called "gunny-sacking" or "stamp collecting." Gunny-sacking sounds something like this: "Now that you've mentioned it, yes, you have done it before. Last July 2nd to be exact, and January 23rd, and April 21st" (Interpretation: "I'm keeping the books and you're in the red."). Of all the collectibles, injuries are the most widely saved and most carefully treasured items because they can be used to exploit the guilt of the offending person.

Every fighter has a belt-line, according to Bach and Wyden, and blows should not be made below the belt; the belt-line is the point above which blows can be absorbed, thereby making them tolerable and fair. Consider this exchange:

> Husband: "Dear, is it necessary to buy the most expensive cologne in the store?"
> Wife: "Humpff! I'm sure you'd spend every last cent to cover up that bald head of yours if you could find a toupee that looks decent!"

Hitting on sensitive areas is punching below the belt. Some "chickens" keep their belts pulled up around their ears, making any kind of criticism seem unjustified and unfair. Disparities in belt-lines are universal. There are limits of tolerance in every fight—a point at which a partner feels he can make no concessions and will no longer negotiate. Intimates can live with a partner's belt-line only if it is openly and honestly displayed, like the honest weight and arm span of the boxer who steps into the ring. It doesn't take living together long to discover the weaknesses of your mate and precisely where and how you can hurt the other if you choose to.

You know what a pinch is—a sudden sharp, painful, and usually unexpected pressure on a sensitive part of your anatomy that makes you recoil and move away. There is an emotional pinch as well as the physical pinch; this is some disturbing word, phrase, or action. Experiences of this kind occur occasionally even in the best relations.

Innuendo and sarcasm make a formidable duo. They are common means to "get at" another. They are special devices for special occasions to produce special responses. We might add ridicule as a particularly vicious tactic. How could anyone who honestly respects his/her mate employ these devices? They are "hit-and-run" tactics. A person who constantly changes his mind in the same argument is fighting dirty. A husband may inform his wife he is prepared to discuss an issue bothering both of them and then he launches into a monologue and never lets her state her views (this sequence is a "warm-up and freeze-up"). Another tactic is to make general indictments and blanket condemnations rather than focusing on specific issues.

Delving into secrets of the past can be devastating. There is one area where less than total candor is diplomatic and this applies to partners who dig and prod for information about outside sexual interests and history and how these partners have responded to them. Boundless tact is necessary. A total statement is not always necessary and while no honest person would advocate deceit, it is true that discretion on the part of both partners is the better part of valor. Herein, discretion may amount to respect for certain topics, for example, the partner's past love affairs or details on intimacy of another marriage.

6. Be As Candid As You Can But Avoid All Pressure Tactics.

Do not shout, strike, clam up, or threaten drastic action. How many mates do you think have threatened or hinted at suicide as a pressure tactic? Women effectively deploy tears, a sign that the female is frustrated, feeling abused, defeated, scared, or too hurt to continue the fight with words. Men are adept at handling this situation and her emotions with the silent treatment. Neither tactic is very productive.

7. Always Temper Differences In Criticism With Appreciation.

In every conflict situation there is some good to report to the mate about his/her attitudes or performance in various roles. Be certain to state these clearly.

8. Don't Try To Win, Ever!

Those who would maintain intimacy in a marriage should be cautioned that "winning" can be more costly than "losing." In boxing, there is a short-term goal: quick victory, preferably by a knock-out. For fights between marriage partners, totally different goals apply. The goal is anything but a knockout. It is, instead, an attempt to improve an over-all relationship for the long-run give-and-take of marriage.

To win an engagement with an intimate enemy may develop into a dangerous situation. It may discourage the loser from leveling in future fights; it may turn him into a devious, camouflaged fighter.

Note: the only way to win intimate encounters is for both partners to win. Illogical as it may sound, one can sometimes win by losing, by not pressing a point or by "rubbing in" an exposed fallacy or error. In constructive marital conflict both partners win the argument. That is, the relationship is improved and therefore both of you benefit from the fight.

9. Confess Your Role In Any Wrong-Doing And Offer Immediate Forgiveness Whenever Wrong-Doing Is Confessed To You.

The Christian places a great emphasis on confession. "Confess your faults one to another and pray one for another" is Biblical counsel that applies as much to marriage as any other relationship. Honest confession is one of the greatest therapies available, though perhaps, some things could be confessed to God alone. There is a place for both individual, private prayer and for duet prayer in a Christian marriage. (In chapter 27 we will be discussing forgiveness.)

10. Always Keep Wholeness And Reconciliation As Primary Goals In Your Marriage Relationship.

Only our sinful pride opens up countless occasions for resentment and hostility. For a Christian there should be a greater urgency to resolve any problems that threaten the continuation of the union. There are many scriptures that teach forgiveness and urge reconciliation. The Christian husband and wife who feel the grace of God in their lives will be drawn to God in prayer, will find it imperative to be reconciled to one another, will find it easier to forgive each other and thus leave the fault-finding and final judging to God.

Jesus taught us that reconciliation involves the restoration of a relationship to all that it can be and he gave guidelines for achieving genuine reconciliation (cf. Matt. 5:23-24; 18:15-17). Reconciliation is always your move first, either way that the wrong was perpetrated or that the hurt developed. In many ways, the key to conflict management is found in the avoidance of blame. Jesus characteristically sought reconciliation without trying to discover who was to blame. He knew enough about human nature to realize that any of us can always make a good case for our own blamelessness. Jesus often warned his hearers that self-righteousness is such a dangerous privilege.

Ultimately, conflict resolution between you and your partner comes down to the heart condition of the two of you. Who is Lord of your life—Jesus Christ or Self? Who determines the values of your life? Who directs the passions of your life? Who is in control of your emotions? Who directs your thoughts and empowers your will? Who lives in you and whose image do you reflect? These are the central questions. "Let there be no more foul language, but good words instead—words suitable for the occasion, which God can use to help other people. Never hurt the Holy Spirit. He is, remember, the personal pledge of your eventual full redemption. Let there be no more resentment, no more anger or temper, no more violent self-assertiveness, no more slander and no more malicious remarks. Be kind to each other, be understanding. Be as ready to forgive others as God for Christ's sake has forgiven you" (Eph. 4:29-32, Phillips). The answer to marital conflict, as you see, is a spiritual one first of all.

Prayer In Duet

Dear Father, as you have given the human family your loving attention, may we give positive attention to each other in our marriage. Help us to know that courtesy, politeness, sharing, doing things for each other, enjoying each other's companionship, and expressing happiness and love are like preventive medicine. Give us the wisdom to discriminate between petty and important issues, to choose our words carefully, to place trust in each other's intentions, and to accept joint responsibility for everything that happens. Forgive us of our sins against you and against one another. Make our marriage whole and may we make the most of the time we can spend with each other. Through Jesus your Son. Amen.

Chapter Nineteen

Does TA Have Anything To Say About Christian Marriage?

The popular theory of psychology called Transactional Analysis may be useful in helping us understand the patterns of interaction in our marriage.

Transactional Analysis (TA) has become a useful tool for many couples working to improve their marriages. It is both a theory of personality and a theory of interpersonal communications. You can use TA to understand the persons and situations in your family and in your social life for it provides insight into the interactions we all experience. TA also provides a language which is useful in discussing these interactions. Since we are serious about improving Christian marriages, a basic understanding of the methodology and language of TA should be helpful. And that is the purpose for including this chapter. Since TA is quite popular you may know already the basic concepts and vocabulary; in which case you might want to skip this chapter and move on to the next topic. If you want to learn more about TA you might read Eric Berne's *Games People Play,* Thomas A. Harris, *I'm OK—You're OK,* and/or James and Jongeward, *Born To Win.*

Psychiatrist Eric Berne originated Transactional Analysis in 1958. Berne developed his theories as he observed how a person's behavior changed when a new stimulus, such as a word, sound or gesture, entered the person's perceptual field. These changes involved tone of voice, posture, facial expressions, and kinds of sentences used; therefore, Berne concluded that different inner people seemed to be in control at different times. Berne theorized that all of us have different *ego states* in our personality. Three ego states appear over and over again in our personalities—the Parent, the Adult, and the Child. The figure below shows how the ego states of the personality are diagrammed.

Ⓟ
Ⓐ
Ⓒ

111

TA theorists suggest that the best way to understand the human brain is to consider it as a highly sophisticated computer which switches on sometime before we are born and switches off the moment we die. Every event of our lives and the accompanying emotional responses are recorded in this computer. The Child's program is written basically within the first 18-24 months of life. Child tapes consist of organismic responses to basic instincts—fear, anger, hunger, thirst, sex, curiosity—or feeling states. These tapes stay with us the rest of our lives and constitute about half of our personality. Parent tapes are the cultural and social information transmitters; they are the source of personal and prejudicial information which are written mostly in the first five to seven years of life. Everything the child saw his parents do and everything he heard them say is recorded in the Parent. For the most part these tapes are controlling, critical and restrictive. Child tapes sound like "I want. . . ." or "I feel. . . ." and Parent tapes sound like "I should. . . ." or "I must. . . ."

The Adult is the data-processing part of the computer which turns out decisions after computing the information from three sources: the Parent, the Child, and the data which the Adult has gathered and is gathering. The Adult is the part that is plugged into reality. The Adult in us listens, reviews, evaluates, and makes rational decisions. The Adult's testing of Parent data may begin at an early age. For example, a secure adolescent is one who finds that most Parent data is reliable: "My parents told me the truth!"

Each ego state can operate positively or it may operate in ways that are destructive and unpleasant to you or to your marriage. When people are in the Child ego state they are thinking, feeling, and acting as they did when they were little children. This can be healthy and rewarding as when both you and your mate have a basic human urge for closeness and intimacy as well as autonomy and freedom. Isn't it great to feel the freedom to be impulsive, creative, inquisitive, to be able to laugh and cry like a naturally free child? When people are in the Parent ego state, they are thinking, feeling, and acting as their parents once did. In the Parent are recorded all the rules, laws, admonitions, and warnings that the person learned from his/her parent figures. If the Parent ego state is well informed by Christian values and ethics there is no doubt that its role as conscience and guardian could be helpful; however, most TA theorists attribute a great many personality disorders to the Parent tapes. When marriage partners are in the Adult ego state they tend to be mature and rational in their decision-making, not locked into beliefs of the past and not bound by what their parents declared a marriage "should" be.

Transactional Analysis constructs the following classification of the four possible life positions held with respect to oneself and others:

1. I'M NOT OK—YOU'RE OK. This is the first tentative decision of the child based on the experiences of the first year or more of life. Psychologists claim that the child, by virtue of his/her small size and helplessness, inevitably considers himself/herself inferior to the adult figures in the social environment.

2. I'M NOT OK—YOU'RE NOT OK. If the child does not receive adequate stroking during the early years, he/she may feel hopelessly abandoned. This person simply gets through life but does not really live. If a person concludes all other people are "NOT OK," he/she will reject stroking, genuine though it may be, and gradually move to a state of extreme withdrawal from the social environment.

3. I'M OK—YOU'RE NOT OK. This is a criminal position that is developed through the experience of abusive and brutal parents. Psychopaths usually occupy this position and have had a history of gross physical abuse. A person with this position always blames others for what happens; such a person may appear to have no conscience about wrongdoing.

4. I'M OK—YOU'RE OK. Here is a position that gives us hope. There is a qualitative difference between this position and the three previous positions. The first three are unconscious, having been made early in life. I'M NOT OK—YOU'RE OK came first and for many people persists throughout life; for certain unfortunate people this position is changed into the second or third position. These first three positions are based on feeling. This fourth position is based on thought, rational choice, and faith. We do not drift into this position—it is a decision we make and a decision we live by.

If you want to analyze your marriage in order to enhance its strengths and work on its weaknesses, TA just might give you some tools of insight and a functional vocabulary for change. Determining your life position can help you understand why you feel about yourself and others as you do. Sorting out ego states can be helpful in understanding your own personality and that of your marriage partner. Additionally, as Christians, we can bring to bear a Biblical perspective to TA theory. For example, the Christian may proclaim I'M OK—YOU'RE OK based on the proper understanding of God's grace which makes all of who receive Jesus in faith OK. I have counseled with people from Christian homes who attempted rational justification of acts of sexual infidelity. Despite the verbalizing of an Adult position ("My mate does not know of this and no one is being hurt"), the counselee may report feelings of guilt and anxiety over an affair. The anxiety is caused by the Parent tapes playing in the background (we never totally erase them though we may try to ignore and repress them) which remind the Adult that such infidelity is sin.

Our goal as Christians is, of course, to view one another as OK and equally loved and precious in God's estimate because of his bountiful grace and to interact with each other as adults, free of manipulative and self-serving gamesmanship. In loving Christian marriages there is always a sense of basic trust and a willingness to be real and to be vulnerable and let the mate be real and vulnerable. There is a responsible caring without manipulation and exploitation. Neither acts as slave or master, as owner or object to be possessed. Does this describe your marriage?

A Thought For Meditation

Your Adult's approach to the worth of persons, either your marriage partner or other people in your social environment, might be summed up in these words by Thomas Harris:

> "I am a person. You are a person. Without you I am not a person, for only though you is language made possible and only through language is thought made possible, and only through thought is humanness made possible. You have made me important. Therefore, I am important and you are important. *If I devalue you, I devalue myself.* This is the rationale of the position I'M OK—YOU'RE OK. Through this position only are we persons instead of things. *Returning man to his rightful place of personhood is the theme of redemption, or reconciliation, or enlightenment, central to all of the great world religions. The requirement of this position is that we are responsible to and for one another, and this responsibility is the ultimate claim imposed on all men alike.*"

A Brief Glossary Of Transactional Analysis Terms

TRANSACTIONS are the things that people do and say to each other. In a transaction, each person gains something from the exchange and what the partners give and take depends on which ego state is active at the time and the kinds of transactions that go on between them.

GAMES people play are the series of transactions in which one or more players ends up feeling NOT OK. Games are not played for fun, are generally learned in childhood and brought into marriage, and are generally played by people who are seldom aware of what is going on. The games usually involve manipulation with the common dramatic roles—Victim, Persecutor, and Rescuer—played out as minidramas in each game. Psychological games are always unproductive uses of time since people play them to avoid positive action, decision-making, or genuine intimacy.

INTIMACY implies a game-free, open relationship with no ulterior transactions.

STROKE: An important TA word that refers to any kind of recognition. The stroke can be verbal (''Great job, honey!'') or nonverbal (a wink or a touch that says ''I see you and I care for you.'').

WARM FUZZY: A positive, life-affirming stroke.

COLD PRICKLY: A negative stroke given to make the partner feel bad in some way (''You never do anything around the house.'')

SCRIPTS are preplanned productions for the dramas of life, dictating where people go with their lives and how they are going to get there. There are three kinds of scripts—constructive, destructive, and going nowhere. Script analysis is the method of uncovering the early decisions, made unconsciously, as to how life shall be lived.

STAMP-COLLECTING is the process of collecting certain feelings for future ''redemption.'' Stamps are colored (red = anger; brown = hurts; blue = depression; green = guilt; yellow = resentment). A marriage partner, for example, may collect enough ''resentment stamps'' to redeem for one ''guilt-free'' extra-marital affair.

Chapter Twenty

Are We Married "Till Debt Do Us Part?"

With our dollars seemingly worth less each year and economic difficulties mounting everywhere, we must be on guard lest the standard of living we are seeking destroys some deeper values.

You may be wondering why a chapter on economics is included in this book on Christian marriage. The subject may seem rather insignificant when placed beside the issues of the nature of marriage, trust, fidelity, growth, and partnership. Well, first of all, are you aware that the word "economy" comes from the Greek *oiconomia*, which means "householding"? The Greek word reflects one of the oldest ways of thinking about the family: as an economic unit. Of course in contemporary society the work that supports a family usually takes place outside the home so that, even though the family remains a producing unit in some respects, we think of the family more as a *consuming* unit.

The above justification for raising the matter of economics is basically academic in nature. But there is a more important practical reason: far more than most people ever realize or than would ever show up in court records, marriages are destroyed, or at least severely weakened, because of economic factors. Consumption really concerns basic questions: What are human needs? and What are human values? Needs and values are interrelated. There are needs in every family and in every society, but these needs may be intensified or diminished by the values of a culture. In fact, needs can be created. In the American culture of the 19th century, saving rather than consuming was the hallmark of the prudent person. People saved wood and metal scraps, repaired rather than traded-in old machinery, mended clothes, put money under rugs and mattresses, preserved leftover food until the next meal. Today it is different. Through the enormous power of media advertising, combined with the American value of "keeping up with the Joneses" and displaying status symbols, people are impelled toward purchasing, consumption, and striving for happiness through ownership. This development is paradoxical in a nation professing to have a deep religious foundation. In fact, virtually every major religion places materialism in opposition to spiritual values and happiness.

Values are abstract, but money, clothes, housing, food, automobiles, and other goods are concrete—they can be touched, seen, counted, added, and subtracted. Arguments and misunderstandings about money and material things are the stuff of situation comedies, melodramas, and jokes—and of almost everyone's everyday life. Chances are you've experienced occasions or major disagreement with your mate over money management. At times there may seem to be no easy solution to such a hassle. Yet such a squabble can often slowly erode a marriage. Sometimes a quarrel over money actually masks a conflict over something else that is too painful for the two partners to face candidly. While it may often seem that money is the cause of hostility between the wife and husband, solutions are often discovered without increasing the amount of money or goods in question. The conflict is resolved when values are clarified, expectations are changed, roles are redefined, communication skills are sharpened, and joint goals are developed.

What kind of economic problem has your marriage faced? Several are fairly common: the indiscriminate use of credit cards, impulsive shopping sprees, the refusal to stick to a firm budget, overspending for housing, hobbies, vacation, or recreation activities, perhaps even the gambling away of money at cards or the race track, poor investments and over-indebtedness. All easily lead to serious marriage and family economic difficulties. In many marriages, an adult-child interaction continues with one playing the role of an impulsive child, spending with no thought about future needs, and the other playing the role of a controlling parent ("You know you shouldn't have bought that. The last thing in the world we need right now is more stereo equipment.").

How can we know when there are creeping financial problems which later might threaten the stability of our marriage? Here are some financial danger signals:

—Routine payment of only minimum amount due on monthly accounts.

—Use of savings or loans to keep up with monthly bills.

—Use of credit to pay for items usually paid for in cash, e.g., food, clothing, entertainment.

—Dependence on additional income such as overtime or moonlighting to keep up with bills.

—Uncertainty about how much is owed or how much interest is being paid on indebtedness.

In a positive vein, here are some practical suggestions that should be helpful whether you are almost-married, just-married, or not-newly-married.

1. The two of you should clarify your values and goals. As marriage partners you want to get the most out of whatever income you have in terms of what is most important to you. Sometimes established marriages will fall into conflict because the partners have never shared their personal values with each other. Without established family value-goals, family income seems always to be siphoned off for the wrong purposes. Money comes and goes but it does not seem to provide the really important benefits that bring inner satisfaction.

2. Plan your personal and family finances. In the face of rising debts, bankruptcies, and economic uncertainties, such planning is more important than ever before. Without planning, money may become your master (Recall the old saying by P. T. Barnum: "Money is a terrible master but an excellent servant."). Studies have shown that couples which engage in financial planning tend to be motivated by having very strong goals, especially home ownership, education of children, and adequate retirement. Positive, long-term financial plans should be made at the beginning stages of the family life cycle.

3. Acquire some basic economic education. All family members participate in some way in society's economy: they work for money, invest, borrow, spend money for consumer goods. But just as a fish does not understand the full character of the water in which it lives, people are not always aware of an "economy" and how it functions. They see only their individual transactions and even then may not be able to explain who benefits most from these transactions.

In 1983 I was awarded a scholarship to attend the Tennessee Economic Education for Clergy Conference sponsored by the University of Tennessee and underwritten by various companies and corporations. The conference included several days of intensive lecturing and group discussion of economic issues. At times it seemed strange sitting with a diverse group of clergymen in the state listening to lectures on economic history, various theories of inflation, the government's role in economy, labor and management issues, and personal financing. Later it was obvious to me that clergymen, through their sermons and private counseling, are in strategic positions to guide individuals through some extremely difficult personal and family problems that are rooted in ignorance of economic and financing issues. For example, how many people do you know could not explain how interest rates on an automobile loan or a revolving charge account were computed? Obviously, in such situations, ignorance is not bliss!

4. Seek the help of a financial adviser whom both of you respect. The counsel of a disinterested adviser might well prevent a financial disaster. Special counsel is important when one of you wants to make a heavy financial investment and the other feels such an undertaking would be unwise. A heavy financial loss based on poor investment need not end a marriage but it is not likely to be forgotten.

5. Study explicit scriptural teachings on stewardship. You know already that the Bible contains many proverbs, parables, and direct statements about how we should use our resources and what our attitudes should be toward our material possessions. In many ways the Bible shows us that God expects us to take our stewardship seriously. One attitude that is sometimes seen in Christians who have a casual, nonchalant approach to heavy indebtedness is that "the Lord will provide no matter what." But the Lord's provision is based on the right ordering of priorities, the proper attitude toward material goods, and honest and diligent work and planning for the future.

Scriptures For Study And Meditation

This is also why you pay taxes, for the authorities are God's servants, who give their full time to governing. Give everyone what you own him: If you owe taxes, pay taxes; if revenue, then revenue; if respect, then respect; if honor, then honor. Let no debt remain outstanding, except the continuing debt to love one another, for he who loves his fellow man has fulfilled the law (Rom. 13:6-8).

Command those who are rich in this present world not to be arrogant nor to put their hope in wealth, which is so uncertain, but to put their hope in God, who richly provides us with everything for our enjoyment. Command them to do good, to be rich in good deeds, and to be generous and willing to share. In this way they will lay up treasures for themselves as a firm foundation for the coming age, so that they may take hold of the life that is truly life (I Tim. 6:17-19).

But seek first his kingdom and his righteousness, and all these things will be given to you as well (Mt. 6:33).

Chapter Twenty-One

Where Do Our Children Fit In?

God has given us no greater stewardship than the care and nurturance of young life, but children must not be placed at the center of marriage.

Some of life's greatest joys and anxieties come from having children. As the father of three children, I can truthfully say that I would not have missed it for anything! How about you? Is there anything you can think of that is more interesting, more unpredictable, and more growth-producing than being a father or mother? Now this book was not intended to deal with the subject of parenting, but it seems that there is at least one very important point that needs to be emphasized. The point is stated in the above preview—children must not be placed at the center of your marriage.

Americans are now in a period of ambivalence about parenthood. More adults in our society than ever before are asking if they even want to be parents. There are increasing numbers of marriages which are child-free, of single-child families, and of families deferring childbirth until much later in their marriage. These changes have occurred mostly among the young and well-educated, but they point to a trend we may expect to increase in the immediate future.

This has not always been the case, of course. In the colonial and early national days of the United States, children came to take on not only a practical dimension but an almost sacred one. Children came to be seen as basic to the marriage itself. A century ago many preachers proclaimed that the procreation of the human family was the chief reason for marriage; the barren womb was thought to be a curse and a married life without children was considered to be an unlovable and unsatisfactory life. God's command to Adam and Eve to "be fruitful and multiply the earth" was interpreted as binding on husbands and wives in days past. Now we may feel like the earth's inhabitants have pretty well multiplied and we wonder if the Creator might have another command for us.

Parenthood may now be considered a matter of choice due to the widespread acceptance of birth control. Modern contraception means that married partners may not only decide whether to have children, but when to have children. And those decisions are crucially important ones. When a man and woman become parents they both enter a new era of their lives together. Even more than marriage, parenthood signifies adulthood—the final, irreversible end of youthful roles. There can be endless debates on whether or not to have children. But once that first child is born, the question is moot. The decision has been made, either thoughtfully and prayerfully or through default, and a parent must live with that decision. When you think about it, the irrevocable nature of parenthood should humble you. You can become an ex-spouse, but never an ex-parent, for the tie of blood always exist. The bond between parent and child is unbreakable; the relationship is a complex one, involving many emotions and lasting in memory long after the death of the parent or child. The transition from nonparent to a parent role is abrupt, occurring literally overnight. Little wonder that many prospective first-time parents experience a spiritual crisis leading to conversion or spiritual renewal.

Did you (or do you) want children? The vast majority of adults want children. But why? Many of the reasons that existed in the past for having children no longer seem important. The economic motive has not only disappeared for the middle class, but in some respects reversed itself. You have probably seen those frightening estimates of how costly it is to raise one child from birth to age 18. Children once made an economic contribution to the family and provided security for parents in their old age. When children work today they usually do it for "spending money" and "learning experiences" rather than for contributing to total family income. And how many middle-age parents expect their children one day to take care of them, barring bankruptcy of Social Security and welfare agencies? And how important is it to have children primarily for the purpose of continuing the family name?

Most likely you and your mate wanted children because you loved each other and you wanted to see that love shared in new, intimate relationships and perpetuated in your own children. A sociologist might say that having children fulfills ego needs of the parents. This need not imply a selfish motive, but rather that the parents want to give and receive love in a primary relationship. As they grow and mature into adults, children are often seen by the parents as friends, as persons they can turn to even for advice, as persons with whom they can travel, converse, and share activities. Some parents develop relationships with their children and children-in-law that resemble double-dating patterns. If this seems strange, consider that the increased lifespan of this century means that parents live longer after their own children have been raised and left home. What kind of activities do you have (or anticipate) with your adult children and their spouses?

What is the real task of parents in child-rearing? Can we approach parenthood with our goals and purposes clearly defined? Stated in broad terms, you as Christian parents want to nurture your children physically, emotionally, and spiritually and transmit to them, through explicit instruction and through their life experiences, the values and expectations of the society in which they live. You certainly want to help your children achieve a personal state of well-being (emotional and mental health), help them become productive, well-adjusted members of the family of humankind and, most important, guide them in moral decision-making so that their attitudes and behavior will reflect the glory of God. These are the broad, long-term goals of child-rearing from the Christian perspective.

How does all of this translate into short-range goals and decision-making? Well, it certainly does not mean that you would want children to be your little carbon copies. If that is your goal you may one day discover that your grown chidren feel a complete dependency on you and that they are unable to make major decisions without being told what they should do. In simplest terms, your responsibility as parents is to help your children develop moral attitudes and per-sonality traits that will enable them to live successfully in the world without you and without other parental figures. One way to accomplish this is by entrusting your children with responsibility for their own decisions. Another way is by refusing to allow all of your marital fulfillment to be centered in the activities and the togetherness with your children, important as such activities are to you at all times. Also, it is important not to hinder their development by allowing too many of your own emotional pressures or handicaps dictate your policies with your children. In almost all areas of parenting, thoughtful parents can pinpoint tendencies toward some courses of action arising out of their own past experiences and hang-ups. It is so easy to act blindly rather than to make rational choices of policy in dealing with a child.

Please remember two basic conclusions: First, the most important advantage, next to love, that you can give to your children is a background and unforgettable example of happily married parents. Happiness in the home and optimism toward the vicissitudes of life strongly influence children. Remember that the habit of happiness is learned, not inherited.

Second your relationship with your mate is more important than your relationship with your children. You made a life-time commitment to your mate before your children even entered the world and, barring divorce or death, will continue to share in that vital relationship after the children have left your home. The relationship between you and your mate is based on mutual need-satisfaction and mutual dependence; in other words it is a relationship between equals which ideally grows richer and deeper as the years go by. The parent-child relationship is based on the initial physical and emotional dependence of the child and the strength of this relationship peaks and then diminishes as the child develops his/her autonomy over the years. Unfortunately, in many marriages one parent may invest more energy in a relationship with a child than with the husband or wife, thus making the child a substitute spouse; such a child may be over-protected and find it difficult to become independent and mature in other relationships. Often it is not until the last child has matured and left home that the evidence of a neglected marriage relationship is confronted.

This point is well stated by James Dobson: "Children were never meant to be the hub of the family. Their place is on the periphery, sheltered and loved, but respected as children and expected to behave that way. The center of a family is the relationship between the husband and wife. All else revolves around that. In this way, when children leave the family, they can do so with the least disturbance to the family unit. If they are in the center of the cell, they cannot emerge without a serious rupture to the whole. Our function as parents is gradually to make ourselves unnecessary, to equip and to permit the child to orbit the family in ever-widening circles, until he establishes himself in society as a fellow adult." And finally, Hodding Carter is reported to have said: "There are only two lasting bequests we can hope to give our children. One of these is roots; the other, wings."

Scriptures For Comment Or Study

I Samuel 1:8—(Note that Elkanah had two wives, Peninnah and Hannah. We speak today of sibling rivalry but in ancient times there must have been in polygamous marriages such a phenomenon as "spouse rivalry." The occasion of Elkanah's large apportionment of meat to Peninnah was but a reminder to Hannah that she was barren, a fact that Peninnah would not let her forget. The statement made by Elkanah to Hannah was intended to assuage her distress and depression over barrenness and reassure her of her intrinsic value as a wife.) ''Hannah, why are you crying and eating nothing? Why are you so miserable? Am I not more to you than ten sons?''

Deuteronomy 6:6-7—These commandments that I give you today are to be upon your hearts. Impress them on your children. Talk about them when you sit at home and when you walk along the road, when you lie down and when you get up.

Ephesians 6:4—Fathers, do not exasperate your children; instead, bring them up in the training and instruction of the Lord.

Chapter Twenty-Two

Can Jealousy Ever Be Conquered?

In nearly all marriages, some advice for taming the "green eyed monster" should be welcomed.

Here's a hypothetical situation for the women. Say you are married to a clergyman and the two of you are enjoying a church fellowship social on Sunday evening. Your enjoyment ends when you observe your husband and an attractive younger woman have been spending several minutes talking together with animated expressions of mutual fondness. This is the same woman your husband occasionally complimented in your presence and who has dropped by his office unannounced for "counsel" or visiting. You have at least two responses:

1. "Her interest in him confirms my suspicion that she has more than friendship in mind. Does she think I can't see her? Does she think I have no feelings? I never did trust her. His interest in her shows he is dissatisfied with me. She's younger and more attractive than me. Maybe he's grown tired of me. She's so attentive to him, so courteous, so appreciative. No wonder he's turned on by how she lavishes him with attention and making him think he's the greatest preacher in the country. If only she knew him like I do! It's obvious she has no regard for his reputation, or else she would not monopolize his time at a church social. I wonder how long he'll let her keep inventing 'excuses' to drop by his office to see him?"

2. "Her interest in my husband confirms his attractiveness to all kinds of people in this church. His interest in her shows he is alert and alive and that he knows a good looking woman when he sees one. I'm glad he does not feel stifled in his relationships with other people. She's different from me in some ways, which suggests he has some social needs I don't meet. I must consider these needs carefully and find out if I could do a better job of meeting them. Thank God he's found someone to discuss some interests that we don't share at all. I'll just let him tell me what he wants me to know and not instigate any probing."

As these two responses to the same situation show, there can be considerable latitude with regard to how you react to and interpret experiences that trigger the jealousy flash. Nearly all of us have experienced such jealousy flashes. We may have been a little unfair in using the response of a woman to a jealousy situation in the opening illustration; there is some research that shows, folklore to the contrary, that males are jealous as frequently and just as intensely as females.

Have there ever been times you wanted to make a loved one jealous of you? If you have, you have displayed a sign of some immaturity in your love. Some have felt an inner satisfaction if they could induce jealously in a friend or mate, as though they were gathering evidence they were loved or esteemed highly. But if you are an extremely jealous mate, you will make yourself miserable and may succeed in making your mate jealous and resentful. Jealousy is a deadly and self-defeating emotion; it is a serious impediment to the development of security and identity. Jealousy, says psychologist Abraham Maslow, "practically always breeds further rejection and deeper insecurity." And, like a destructive malignancy, jealousy breeds more jealousy.

A definition is in order. In a world of rapid change and capricious chance, all of us are seeking stability and certainty in intimate relationships. Any person who seems to threaten or interfere with an established intimacy becomes a threat. Jealousy is an understandable response to such a threat. Originally, jealousy meant vigilance, solicitude, a watchful zeal, with perhaps a hint of potential wrath, as in Jehovah's declaration and warning, "I the Lord thy God am a jealous God." In our society, jealously is perhaps best defined as suspicion or resentment of someone you consider to be a rival, someone or some situation you fear threatens a relationship you value. The Lord charged Moses to speak a word to the Israelites about husbands who experienced a "fit of jealousy" and directed jealous husbands to appear with their wives before the priest with a prescribed offering (cf. Num. 5:11f).

Jealousy is not the same as envy, though the words are sometimes used as synonyms; indeed, the two do name related emotions and behaviors. Envy stems from the desire to acquire something possessed by another, while jealousy is rooted in the fear of losing something already possessed. Jealousy is concerned with the maintenance of a relationship in the face of an apparent challenge to its continuation. A man may envy a Connors or McEnroe for his skill at tennis. A woman may envy a Lady Diana for her charm and notoriety. But neither is jealousy; neither brings sharp, piercing stabs of emotional pain. The people we envy are not a threat to us; they just happen to possess what we would like to have. The object of marital jealousy is someone who threatens to take away all or part of the mate we love. Jealousy is more than just a word; it is a complex, gut-feeling experience filled with anxiety, fear, resentment, threat, and other hurting emotions. For many it is true that "jealousy is cruel as the grave" (Song of Solomon 8:6).

The essence of jealousy is in our perception of an interpersonal relationship. You do not have to perceive the complete loss of your mate to another in order to feel its sting. No one person can ever "own" another, yet it is easy to convince ourselves that love demands total monopoly of the mate's life and decisions. A husband may lavish his wife's attention and pampering but may become jealous of her if she showers such attention on anyone but him, even their own children. A woman may feel the stirrings of jealousy when her husband finds it necessary to spend extra time working more closely with his secretary. A tone-deaf man may have no use for any but country music, but feel jealous when his wife asks about attending a symphony concert with another person. Profession, clients, hobby, in-laws, children—all can be the catalyst for jealousy when one mate perceives any of them absorbs too much of the mate's time and devotion.

Incidentally, when it comes to conceptualizing jealousy, there is some evidence indicating a sex difference. Men are more apt to deny jealous feelings; women are more apt to acknowledge them. Females tend to be jealous of the time their partners would spend with another woman, or attention that the men would pay to her. Men conceptualize jealously in terms of sexual contact that their partners might be having with other men. One explanation for this sex difference is that men are taught to see their partners as their sexual possessions, whereas women are not. Possessive-jealousy is perhaps the most wrathful and raging form of jealousy, leading to reactions such as cruel vengeance and even murder; that such jealousy is understandable and deemed justifiable is obvious when you consider that juries often acquit men who kill their wives' lovers. Jealous men are more apt to focus on the outside sexual activity of the partner, whereas jealous women are more likely to focus on the emotional involvement between her husband and another woman. Men are more likely to blame "circumstances" for infidelity and then display competitive behavior; women often blame themselves and display possessive behavior.

Regardless, jealousy is not the exclusive trait of either gender, nor is it unique to any one type of culture or age. Jealousy transcends almost all cultural differences and cannot be blamed, as some detractors have suggested, on the standards of Christian ethics or western capitalism. Those who opt for "open marriage" or sexual freedom in pair bonding in order to free themselves from jealousy and other negative emotions of monogamous marriage soon discover a new set of circumstances in which jealousy is even more frequent and intense.

Jealousy, for many of us, may be the most deeply rooted and most difficult to control emotion we ever experience. Why is this true? A psychological explanation would trace jealousy back to infancy and the nearly universal fact that infants are nurtured by, and form primary attachement to, one person. An intimate attachment to another person late in life evokes some of the earlier feelings—the sense of dependency and the wish to be the exclusive recipient of the significant other's love. Jealousy in adult life becomes the equivalent of sibling rivalry in childhood. A sociological explanation is based on the difference between a dyad (two people interrelating) and a group of all other sizes from three on up. Even in a triad, one person can depart and there is a sense of the group carried on by the two others. But in a dyad there is no group independent of the two people; if one person dies or leaves for another, that is the end of the relationship. Thus, the peculiar properties of the dyad make it the most intimate of groups, and hence the most vulnerable to jealousy. The addition of a third party to a two-person group introduces a different structure and changes the relationship between the original pair; the third is always intruder. A theological explanation, of course, would focus on the value of a mutual, irrevocable, life-time commitment.

We have introduced jealousy and tried to explain it as a serious problem. However, you may feel that no practical advice on taming the green-eyed monster has been offered. And here's the rub! Truth is, there's little or nothing that we should attempt in terms of directly controlling our mate's thinking and behavior. Remember, we are only responsible for ourselves. But we are not helpless against the force of this emotion. We might first sort out the various types of jealousy. There is a jealousy that comes from feeling excluded and the more serious variety that we've already discussed, the jealousy from fear of loss. The difference is between a small problem and a large one, between the benign and the malignant.

Do your jealousy flashes come from feeling left out of an activity involving your partner and another person or other people? When your mate pays attention to another, is your first reaction to judge that they are "in" and you are "out?" Do you feel excluded, ignored, unappreciated? These experiences are fairly common in our society and dealing with them gracefully is part of the etiquette of our time. Don't let these experiences obscure the deeper assurances your mate continues to make that you are number one in his/her life. Do you not have similar experiences (or at least the opportunity for same) in which your mate could feel the same reactions?

On the other hand, if you find yourself troubled or upset by having to share your partner in ways usually considered appropriate and in good taste among your circle of friends, your feeling of exclusion may reveal an underlying, neurotic fear of loss. This is the more serious type of jealousy. Can you not stand to let your husband spend a Saturday hunting or fishing? Can you not stand to allow your wife to take an entire day to shop out of town? Can you not let your partner out of your sight? Then your jealousy is probably rooted in a persistent fear rather than a temporary irritation. What does this tell you about yourself? Remember not to confuse commitment with belonging to. Possessiveness is commitment without trust; conversely, commitment with trust celebrates the uniqueness and autonomy of the other.

All types of jealousy are shaped by elements of self-concept and your mood. When you feel good about yourself, you are less likely to feel jealous. If you feel strong and independent-minded, jealousy should not be a serious problem, no matter how your mate behaves. You are more susceptible to this deadly emotion when you are depressed, dissatisfied with yourself, and insecure in your social environment. Your feelings about the third party are also important. If you want to like and consider him/her a worthy friend of both of you, occasional hugs between your mate and friend will hardly be given a second thought. If you want to think evil of the other person, the same gestures will be unsettling, threatening, and provide more basis for biting criticism of the person.

Christian mates should not use jealousy to manipulate each other. This tactic is sometimes accompanied by an appeal to duty: "You owe it to me to stop seeing her." Love must not be treated as a duty. There are many ways to strengthen love, but jealousy is not one of them. No man or woman ever loves his/her mate more because he/she suffered as a victim of jealousy; nor is anyone more faithful in thought or deed who is suspected of being unfaithful.

Jealousy must be dealt with as a serious problem. As such, it has a basic and legitimate function—alerting us to threats to our personal security and to the health of an intimate relationship. As Christian mates, confess jealousy for what it is. ("I love you . . . I want you . . . I'm afraid of what's happening and I need you to help me stop it.") Do not try to camouflage jealousy as solicitousness. When making continual pointed and often petty, critical comments about your mate or his friends or schedule, check to see if jealousy is not at the root of what you are saying. Once confessed, a constructive, in-depth dialogue can lead to a clarification of needs, meanings, beliefs, and values. If jealousy is confessed to you, don't be so presumptuous as to assume that the jealousy is automatically unfounded or unjustified. Do not allow jealousy to degenerate into feelings of guilt, self-pity, or helplessness ("Poor me. I'm not loved anymore!") And when you work through jealousy at one point in your marriage, don't be terrified to see it resurface in another set of circumstances. Your jealousy is neither proof of love nor evidence of personal failure. It is merely a signal which tells you to attend to your relationship and to yourself. Left unquestioned, jealousy remains malevolent. Examined in the light of reason, jealousy can be a stimulus for growth.

Prayer In Duet

Father, we thank you for your love for us and we want to return your love. We know that you as our Heavenly Father are not jealous when men and women give themselves to each other. May the love of the two of us be deep enough and strong enough to transcend jealousy. May we know that agapic love provides the inner power both to be happy for others as well as self and to rejoice in the successes and achievements of others. We do not experience all of each other's intimate friendships, but we rejoice and praise you for the persons we are and in the richness of our relationships. Help us to discover new ways to communicate our love to each other that will be reassuring and comforting. Through Jesus. Amen.

Chapter Twenty-Three

How Open Should Our Marriage Be?

In every marriage some careful thought should be given to the issues of separateness and special friendships outside of marriage.

You've probably heard a lot of sermons and lectures at church on the nature of the "ideal" marriage and, of course, one of the major components of this much romanticized lifestyle has been togetherness—togetherness of the couple and togetherness of the family. Your family is my family, your interests are my interests, your needs are my needs, your leisure time is my leisure time, your friends are my friends. So goes the ideal that the church in its concern for marital commitment has strongly endorsed. To buttress this ideal view of marriage preachers have frequently read the familiar pledge of Ruth to Naomi, "Whither thou goest, I will go; whither thou lodgest, I will lodge; thy people shall be my people . . ." Does this describe your view of marriage? Is it possible that such a marriage style could be stifling? When we instruct our children to search for mates who will share all their interests and have all their tastes, are we teaching them unrealistic goals for a marriage relationship? Does such a romantic ideal of marriage almost excuse its participants from the necessity of being whole persons?

Marriage is a paradox in the sense that "two become one" and yet each remains a separate creature for God, uniquely created and free for God. We have spoken already of how two become one through sustained intimacy at all levels of life together, beginning with the spiritual level. But unity might be a better term than union when the latter connotes a submergence of the personality and uniqueness of one or both partners. In the poetic sense we employ the concept of "two becoming one," but outside the sphere of poetry it would literally mean the annihilation of one and probably both people. While we in the church have emphasized the first half of the paradox of marriage, we have often failed to affirm the other half of the paradox, namely that while the two belong to each other in love, they need also to remain two separate creatures of God.

At times the folklore of our culture seems wiser than the well-meaning counsel offered by parents and friends. "Opposites attract," according to an old folk saying; this indicates a marriage can tolerate considerable diversity since the relationship began in diversity. And you have heard many times the old saying "Variety is the spice of life." The problem in a highly structured and closed marriage is that all differences are a little threatening somehow and that differences of interest smack of selfishness. Sometimes differences in values are totally suppressed. And to suggest that more spice could be added to a closed marriage structure would be tantamount to recommending extramarital affairs.

In a more open marriage style, the values of individuality and separation are allowed expression. To people indoctrinated with the idea that you help others by closeness and nurturing support, separateness and individuality may seem like desertion or indifference. You, too, may be startled by the idea that you and your mate can remain separate creatures of God with your own interests, your own hobbies, your own friends, and your own personalities and yet be one. But rather than being a threat, the more individual experiences, interests, and peripheral relationships that each of you can incorporate into your own marital unity, the more you can enrich and strengthen your marriage. You are bringing more to your marriage because you have more to share. There is no suggestion here about extramarital affairs. Surely there is spicy variety enough in any married couple, but only if the two are willing to risk claiming and developing their separate individuality.

The major focus of this book has been interpersonal relationships as they develop and function within marriage and the family setting. But here we must raise the question of how interpersonal needs are met outside the family. All people need friends with whom they can be intimate; neither individuals nor marriages can function well when they exist in isolation.

You have certain needs that can only be met in relationships with other people:

1. Nurturance needs: this need is filled through caring for a partner, children, or other intimates both physically and emotionally.

2. Social needs: You need to feel actively involved in some form of community, lest you feel isolated or bored.

3. Assistance needs: You need to know that if something bad happens to you, there are people you can rely on for help, lest you feel anxious and vulnerable.

4. Intimacy needs: You need people who will care about you and listen to you, lest you feel emotionally isolated and lonely.

5. Reassurance needs: You need people to respect your skills as

a person, parent, partner, and worker, lest you lose your self-esteem.

Ideally, these needs will be met in your marriage and within your family structure as a whole. Could you not conclude that if most of your deep personality needs are not met by your partner, then something is wrong with your marriage relationship? On the other hand, it may be difficult to have all these needs met all the time or even part of the time within the family. You husbands may find that your wives have little or no interest in racketball, professional football, golf, baseball, carpentry, auto repair, and motorcycling and may not respect your skills in these areas. And you wives may find that your husbands have little or no interest in sewing, cooking, bridge, classical music, needlework, home decoration, P.T.A., and ceramics and may not respect your skills in these areas.

All of us usually need further support for our values, activities, labor and even leisure interests. It does not matter if yours is the best marriage possible, it cannot meet all of your needs. Your husband or wife may meet many of your needs, share many of your pleasures, validate your worth, sustain your interests; but because each person is unique, there are many aspects of yourself that you do not share with your mate. You can be intimate with your friends in ways you are not with your mate; discuss ideas your mate might find ridiculous; laugh about situations your mate finds humorless. Friendship is significant for the full development of our marriages and ourselves. There is a Spanish saying, *"La vida es corta, pero ancha,"* which simply means, ''Although life is all too short, it can be ever so wide.''

Friends come from many sources. You make friends with people with whom you share similar ideas, activities, and values. These similarities provide the basis for openness and eventually intimacy, the sharing of ourselves at the deepest levels. One important source of friends is our relatives. Mothers and sisters may be especially important as confidants while men tend only to be close to their brothers (one study shows that very rarely do fathers become confidants of their married children). Because they are more mobile geographically and socially, middle-class husbands and wives are less likely to have as many relatives who are also friends. Friends also come from childhood friendships, college classmates, co-workers, church members, and neighbors. When people marry, they often lose a number of friends, especially those of the opposite sex whose friendship may be perceived as a threat by the new wife or husband.

Are there any significant differences between the friendships formed by women and the ones formed by men? Well, some research is available on this question. The evidence strongly suggests that the friendships of women are more frequent, more significant, and more interpersonally involved than those commonly established by men. Friendships among women are commonly based on trust and involve much more revealing of the self to the other. Close friendships among women are generally defined as ones which are self-revealing, spontaneous, and accepting, whereas close friendships between men are subjectively defined in terms of doing things together. Women's friendships tend to deal with inward-feeling things while men's friendships are more outwardly directed and less feeling. The evidence supports the conclusion that women can form friendships easier than men and that women not only have more close friends than men but they also reveal more about themselves.

We come now to the most difficult issue to be raised in this chapter: How do you feel about cross-sex friendships outside of marriage and outside the extended family? Put another way, how do you feel or how would you feel about your husband or wife having a close friend of the opposite sex? Perhaps you have a firm answer to this question already. Or before answering the question you might ask, "Just how close?" Obviously, the Seventh Commandment of the Decalogue and the clear teaching of the New Testament commit us to faithfulness to our sexual vows. But, as we shall see later, fidelity is an ideal so rich and flexible that we may always seem to be in a quandary when making decisions about the numerous possibilities of relationships between married men and women. And the Bible has no explicit statement on the subject nor does it give us an example of such a friendship. Do you think that all married people are safe in their relationships outside of marriage so long as they do not commit the act of adultery? Or are all close friendships with a member of the opposite sex a subtle failure in marital fidelity? It seems to me that only a legalist would answer yes to the first question and no to the second.

The more that our intellectual and emotional needs become complex and the more that men and women are placed together almost as equals in various occupational and career settings, the more this issue becomes important in marriages of all kinds. But the issue is one that you and your mate must resolve for yourselves and what seems to work for other couples may or may not work for you. In resolving this issue, if it has not been done already, you might consider the following points:

1. There are a number of barriers to cross-sex relationships. If you or a married acquaintance believes such a relationship is wrong, shameful, or threatening to significant others, then the chances of a close friendship are going to become seriously restricted. If you

attempt to develop an intimate relationship with someone who is uncomfortable with it you may only borrow trouble and heartache. We are not speaking simply about the dangers of sexual entanglements; there are many good Christians who believe that a relationship with the opposite sex is socially and personally demeaning, indiscreet, or wrong and such a conviction terminates many possible cross-sex friendships at an early stage.

2. Cross-sex friendships are almost always sexually-tinted. It is commonly assumed that a woman and man may develop a sexual relationship *without* any degree of friendship. However, whether there can be friendship without some degree of sexual interest and involvement would be much less agreed on. Do you agree that it is nearly impossible to remove the specter of sexuality from the close friendship of any normal adult male and female? The attractiveness you have for others and that you feel in others of the opposite sex is simply a part of the way that God made you. We state this point, not to claim that such friendships are wrong, but in order to be realistic about the dimensions and dynamics of such friendships.

3. Cross-sex friendships are risky. The risk grows out of the escalating experience of mutual self-disclosures of two friends of the opposite sex. If a man and woman have some dependency on each other and if they continue to share in the mystery of each other, all of which is basic to friendship, they will almost inevitably find it easy to depend on each other in the sexual area. Once the door is opened to sharing needs, yearnings, unfulfilled desires, it may be difficult to stop the emotional flow that leads to ultimate intimacy.

4. Cross-sex friendships can be especially threatening to the mates involved. When a married man/woman devotes so much time and energy to an outside relationship, the mate(s) involved may feel robbed of prime time and high level energy. Such a friendship often implies to others that something must be missing from their respective marriages because it is generally assumed that couples will get all they need in cross-sex intimacy from their spouses.

5. Cross-sex friendships can be consistent with marital fidelity but do require discretion. We might recall that Jesus was blessed by the love and support of a special group of women in his company of disciples. Circumstances and persons are intricately woven so as to make each friendship unique. Our faith should be that God can make each friendship we pursue and develop an instrument of blessing for each person. God graciously gives us the gift of friends and our lives are blessed when we receive and exercise this gift with moral responsibility, integrity, honor, and discretion.

An Exercise For The Two Of You

1. List on paper eight or ten of the ways in which you and your-mate are different. Include values, personality differences, tastes, general outlook, hobbies, and skills.

2. Discuss with each other how you feel about these differences. What would you like to do about them?

3. Which of these differences do you try to resolve? How do you resolve them? Which differences do you just accept and why?

4. List also the friends, either male or female, that you have that your mate does not have. Discuss what added dimension to your life or marriage each important friendship brings to the two of you.

5. Go back over your list of differences and list of friends and after each one write down the challenge that is represented for you. (It might be the challenge of acceptance, the challenge to quit offering unwanted advice, the challenge of looking at yourself and others differently, etc.)

A Thought For Meditation

But let there be spaces in your togetherness,
And let the winds of the heavens dance between you.
Love one another, but make not a bond of love:
Let it rather be a moving sea between the shores of your
    souls.
Fill each other's cup but drink not from one cup.
Give one another of your bread but eat not from the same
    loaf.
Sing and dance together and be joyous, but let each of you
    be alone,
Even as the strings of a lute are alone thought they quiver
    with the same music.
Give your hearts, but not into each other's keeping.
For only the hand of Life can contain your hearts.
And stand together yet not too near together;
For the pillars of the temple stand apart,
And the oak tree and the cypress grow not in each other's
    shadow.

from *The Prophet,* by Kahil Gibran

Chapter Twenty-Four

What About Sex?

Here's everything you wanted to know about sex (well, more modestly, here's a lot of what you wanted to know about sex), but were afraid that you wouldn't hear from the home pulpit.

If you were to judge by the media, it would seem that there is little sex within marriage. On the television there is five times as much sex between unmarried partners as between married ones. Married men have sex more often with prostitutes than with their wives. Erotic activity is frequently linked with violence. And sexual research is not much different from the entertainment media. There are literally hundreds of studies on premarital sexuality, extramarital sexuality, homosexuality, and sexual variations, but, by comparison, almost nothing exists on marital sexuality. You may be among those wondering, "What is it that makes for good sex in marriage?"

All of us have been touched by the sexual revolution in one way or another. You and your mate may be trying "to get your act together" on this subject. You may have looked for a healing word from the church (from your preacher or your elders or a teacher) and been greeted by silence—a silence that grows out of fears, ignorance, shame, and hang-ups. If you know anything about Christian sex ethics, you know that marital sexuality is intended to be monogamous. Even if you had premarital sex with several partners, you knew that once you were married all sexual interactions were expected to take place between you and your mate. This expectation and commitment last a lifetime. Think about it: a person marrying at 20 commits himself/herself to 60 or 70 years of sex with the same person. This is a radical goal and a radical ethic which, of course, not everyone keeps. But the radical ethic is rooted in the possibility of fidelity to a radical commitment.

How do you manage such a commitment in terms of normal sexuality? This chapter is only a listing of ten general statements on the subject of sex for Christians. An entire book could be written on the subject; in fact, several good books have already been published. The general points are in no special order and are stated only briefly in hope that you and your partner will discuss them and draw out the implications for your own marriage.

1. As Christians we believe that sex is a gift from God to be received in gratitude and to be enjoyed in the mystery of goodness and ecstasy.

Human sexuality is rooted in the creation narrative. Our bodies are part of the Creator's design; God created us with femaleness and maleness. Enjoying sex in marriage on a regular basis is to celebrate what God has done for us and what he has given us.

Animals engage in sexual behavior, but for humans sex is not simply and solely instinctual. Only humans can stand in self-conscious relationships with their Creator and with one another. And both sexes are mutually essential to each other in order to effect completeness. Dust and divinity are imparted to the nature of man as male and female so that sexuality is:

a. Partly chemical and earthy (involving glands and chemicals)
b. Partly animal (involving basic drives; mammals have similar drives)
c. Partly, even largely, psychological (involving our wills, values, etc.)

Would it be overstating it to say that sex in marriage can be sacramental, an outward sign and behavior signifying an inner covenant made to one another and to God? Perhaps this is one facet of the mystery that Paul discusses in his letter to the Ephesians. Much truth is spoken in the old maxim that the chief sex organ of the human is the brain. Thus sex can be lifted to a spiritual plane. Ultimate sexual relations between a Christian man and Christian woman committed to one another may be called a psychosoma-pneumatic (soul-body-spirit) union.

2. Christians should have no shame or guilt about their bodies or the union of bodies in sex, because God has blessed our lives by making sex such a powerful, pervasive drive in all normal humans.

"However much sex may be banalized in our society," writes Rollo May, "it remains the power of procreation, the drive that perpetuates the race, the source at once of man's most intense pleasure and his most pervasive anxiety. It can, in its daimonic form, hurl the individual into sloughs of despond, and, when allied with eros, it can lift him into orbits of ecstasy." We might wish that sex were not such a powerful motivator in human relationships, but it is. Do you ever feel that your keen interest in sex and your delight in sexual pleasure is anything but utterly normal and healthy? What is unhealthy is the repression of sexual interest and curiosity. And we might recall the counsel of St. Augustine who said, "We must not be ashamed to talk about what God was not ashamed to create."

There is a flip side to this point: Sexual drives are not always as powerful as we imagine. Sex needs are not on the same level and hardly have the same urgency as needs for food, water, shelter and clothing. Sexual responsivity can be delayed indefinitely or functionally denied for a lifetime. Furthermore, what may be more powerful than our sex drives may be the feelings that accompany them. We feel love, tenderness, guilt, anxiety, security, aggression and even contempt in association with our sex drives. We may misread the physiological event when we experience one or more of these intense emotions during sexual behavior; we may identify the emotional intensity with the physical act.

3. As Christians we turn to the Bible for guidance in the area of sexuality, but we must use the Bible wisely and carefully.

To what passages do we turn for direction about our sexuality? Obviously, the Bible does not give systematic teaching on sex in all its categories. The various Biblical authors always wrote in response to the needs and conditions of their own historical situations. When you read the Old Testament, you must keep in mind that in most ancient cultures women were considered to be property, a view which sanctioned the double standard. The timeless teaching of Jesus on marriage was delivered largely to legalistic Jews. Paul spoke eloquently of marriage to the Ephesians but to the Corinthians he spoke with an urgency and sense of impending doom for the current age and thus he counseled against marriage except in the case of excessive sexual appetite.

Additionally, the Bible says nothing about the etiquette of courtship and sex manners. You will find nothing in the Bible on sexual dysfunction. Jesus had a high estimate of marriage but did not himself marry and nothing is said of the women in the lives of his selected apostles. In I Corinthians 7, Paul speaks of sexual sharing as a mutual responsibility in marriage but you would not pick up from him any hint that sexual union is a gateway to personal fulfillment and voluptuous ecstasy. On the other hand, there is at least one clear endorsement of sexual passion in the Scriptures and there is no other way to interpret the Song of Solomon than as a healthy celebration of erotic love (see also Prov. 5:18-19).

What the Bible does offer is some very clear principles on how we should relate to others as well as some clear prohibitive commands. To borrow the language of Martin Buber, the New Testament advocates I-Thou relationships and condemns I-It relations. The Christian will not dominate and manipulate others as a mere means to satisfy his/her sexual desires. Casual sex, defined as sex apart from lasting commitment, is therefore spurned. Christian values and norms inform and shape your sexual behavior. It is not sexual behavior that determines character so much as it is character that determines sexual behavior. Put another way, character (the system of values and philosophy by which you live) is what determines the particular ways in which you handle and satisfy your sexual drive.

4. Human sexuality finds its meaning in the context of love and commitment.

Sexual fulfillment was your natural and joyful expectation when the two of you were a newly married bride and groom. But if you have achieved fulfillment, it did not just happen. When sexual intercourse is defined as a lovemaking, meaning the simple act of giving and receiving love, then persons with those abilities are presupposed. And this love that the couple share with each other must be reinforced by a considered, responsible commitment. If either partner is not committed to give herself or himself fully to the other, sexual union is certainly possible but may become superficial. Under circumstances without love and commitment, it is possible for two people to participate mechanically in sexual intercourse, but they never really "give" or "accept" the experience and they may never be "close" to one another, even when their bodies are interlocked.

If your relationship is not loving and open, sex is not a genuine expression of love. When sex is used for proving adequacy, releasing tension, or creating the illusion of intimacy, it eventually becomes routine and boring. You may then think you have to learn how to respond, what buttons to push, what areas to touch, or how to talk to each other. But, when there is no real love and commitment, techniques can only lead to unsatisfying, routine experiences and the search might continue for new techniques or new partners to ignite passion. You may read books, have therapy, talk to friends or attend classes in a quest to be orgasmic. While being informed sexually is important, you can never learn to create passion through the skillful manipulation of bodies. Continuing passion and desire result from intimacy based on mutual commitment and shared feeling.

Marriage is the consummation of a deepening relationship of love and personal commitment while, similarly, sexual union is the consummation of a growing physical intimacy. In God's design, the two consummations converge at the point of marriage. Since the sexual relationship is the most intimate, the most personal, the most profound physical relationship that can be established between two human beings, its fulfillment is realized within the security of a lifetime commitment of sexual exclusiveness to the other. You can say to your partner, "Because I can never do anything more intimate than this with anyone, I am yours and yours only in the most intimate possible union. And our sexual intimacy is both substantive and symbolic—substantive in the sense that the pleasure is real and symbolic in its representation of our emotional intimacy."

5. Sex is not an end in itself but is a gift of God given to us to serve more valuable ends.

a. Reproduction/Procreation

This purpose of sex is so obvious. Who knows but what perhaps God threw in pleasure for a catalyst in the human reproduction system to make certain the earth was populated. But, of course, this is not the sole function. Only 1/1000 or less of sexual experiences in marriage have to do with reproduction.

b. Communication

Traditionally, the English word "intercourse" meant communication and only recently took an exclusively sexual connotation. Even the term "sexual relations" implies that sex is more than a function; it is relationship. Elton Trueblood writes: "One of the most significant things to say about sexual intercourse is that it provides husband and wife with a language which cannot be matched by words or by any other act whatsoever. Love needs language for its adequate expression and sex has its own syntax." As we know, words lend themselves to corruption; the body has a more primitive unsophisticated mode of expression.

The Old Testament explicitly points to sexual intercourse as an experience in communication, for the Hebrew term is translated "to know" (Gen. 4:1). In coitus, the man discovers what it really means to be a male and through her experience with a man the female knows what it is like to be a woman. Intercourse means involvement and participation with a loved one in an experience calculated to reveal something of each one's true identity; something of the mystery of another is revealed. This profound sharing cannot be fully appreciated by those who have barely passed puberty.

c. Pleasure

What normally married person can deny this? Pleasure is God's bonus for your uniting act. A satisfying sex life releases tension, renews tired spirits (even if it makes you sleepy), and offsets the heartaches and failures of human existence. Sex is a favorite way to drop the load of adult responsibilities and parenting duties and to let your inner child play again. The fullness of pleasure is experienced when you and your mate engage in the most intimate behavior possible, free of exploitation and free of the violation of the will or integrity of another person or of the Lord's purpose and untainted by any guilt. How sad it is when Christians believe that sex is not to be enjoyed for pleasure but is to be endured and to occur as demand and obligation! Let's enjoy it and make no apology for it.

6. Your mood can determine both your sexual pleasure and your sexual ability.

The human is the only animal in which emotional states affect sexual functioning. In both male and female, thought or memory may influence glandular and emotional reactions. Consequently, conflicts over children, money or religion, neglect or discourtesies, quarrels and bitter words will all have their effect in the marital bed. If you fail in your marriage relationships, it is possible that you will fail in sexual relations. When a couple tells a counselor that their chief problem is sex, the problem is not usually with sex but with the two people.

There is a right time and right place for sex. But when you or your partner brings to bed a set of long standing hang-ups, repressed emotions, inhibitions, or frustrations, then you may expect more frustration between the sheets.

7. Good sex cannot save a troubled marriage, but a troubled marriage may experience the symptom of a troubled sexual relationship.

It is important to understand that sexuality is but one aspect of marriage. Sometimes we expect too much of sex. The union of two bodies cannot create love—prostitution proves this. Furthermore, the frequency of sexual intercourse does not always determine the marital happiness or sexual satisfaction. Less sex does not mean bad sex. High frequency of intercourse and orgasm does not guarantee sexual satisfaction. After intercourse, for example, you may feel sad, angry, alientated, guilty, used, or helpless as well as happy, close, joyful, peaceful, and intimate. Your meaning for the sexual act is found in you and your mate, not in the act itself.

8. Sex will function naturally in your marriage when it is "lived" rather than "performed."

Are you interested in a "super sex" life? Well, it comes as a result of the atmosphere that has been carefully created all day. There are so many sex manuals in the bookstores today and just to browse through them you get the impression that great sex is a matter of mastering technique and becoming a sexual athlete. There is a value to some of the manuals when you discover ideas and information not learned elsewhere. But great sexual experiences come to those whose emotional bonding is strong and who are willing to maintain continuing romance.

Sensuality and eroticism go together. People are born sensory creatures—hearing, seeing, tasting, touching, smelling—a part of being human. To be sensuous is to be susceptible to the senses and to feel pleasure through them. Some Christians try to avoid sensuousness. They do not enjoy their bodies; in fact, they seem embarrassed to have them. They may expect their bodies to function like machines that do not need attention.

Touching and being touched can be a most effective sensuous "turn on" for most people. Some like to be fondled, some do not. Some like gentleness, some like roughness. Some prefer certain parts of their bodies to be touched and not other parts. Have you discovered sensuality in your marriage? Do you know how to communicate through touch? Are you aware of the role of hygiene in sexuality? of the value of certain scents? items of clothing?

"Don't touch!" is a lesson learned early in life and is deeply ingrained. Psychologists know that tactile stimulation is an essential element in a baby's development. Adolescents have a need and at least moderate interest in touching and being touched; pleasurable sensations flow through the fingertips moving across flesh that is different from one's own. Once a sexual relationship in marriage is established most couples may use touch as a nonverbal signal of willingness. Some men even regard it as a waste of time and effort, an unnecessary postponement of intercourse. Even adults need an affectionate reaching out to other adults. This does not have to be a sexual come-on. Four hugs a day will help you survive the blues but a dozen is better, according to Virginia Satir; "our pores are places for messages of love," she claims. Masters and Johnson have written several articles on the need for adult touching: "For the man and woman who value each other as individuals and who want the satisfactions of a sustained relationship, it is important to avoid the fundamental error of believing that touch is a means to an end. It is not. *Touch is an end in itself.* It is a primary form of communication, a silent voice that avoids the pitfall of words while expressing the feelings of the moment. It bridges the physical separateness from which no human being is spared, literally establishing a sense of solidarity between two individuals." Touching nourishes the pleasure of being alive and satisfies the profound creature need not to feel alone. There is great joy in being touched and in touching another trusted and trusting person of the opposite sex.

In this connection, the art of creative snuggling is recommended. The mastery of this art may prove life-prolonging in the less passionate senior years. A common complaint is, "My husband (or wife) is never affectionate unless it is for sex." Most couples would not have this problem if they solved their bedtime snuggling problem. Creative snuggling is not feasible in twin beds (unless one of the beds is abandoned).

9. Sexual intimacy (a sharing in the joy of being in the presence of one another) is not the same as sexual fidelity.

Many couples claim they are committed to sexual fidelity, yet there may be little or no sexual intimacy in their relationship. Maintenance of intimacy may hinge on freedom to be playful, experimental, and adventuresome in sex.

Sex rituals, no matter how desirable and comfortable, should be kept open for revisions, repeals and amendments; the routines must be kept negotiable via clear cues or commands. This is effective insurance against monotony. More insurance is the extension of sex beyond the bedroom. A sound psychological case can be made against exclusive use of the bed for location of affection and intercourse. Bed is where people go to be lazy, sick, tired, infantile, and eventually to die. Obviously the bed is convenient and comfortable but, given sufficient privacy, sex can be more stimulating in unusual places.

Your sex rituals tend to be well routinized as the years go by. Established sex mates know what to look for from the first stereotyped touch of erotic foreplay. Also, your language tends to be the same. Remember that a little variety is the spice of life. Some Christian couples are concerned about vulgar language and about certain forms of sexual expression, especially oral sex. A rule I offer in sexual counseling is that anything which is:

(a) physically enjoyable
(b) emotionally satisfying
(c) mutually agreeable

is morally right! What do you think?

10. Sex problems may be expected over the long tenure of marriage.

Your marriage may have begun with difficulty. Oscar Wilde once commented that Niagara Falls is the second greatest disappointment of an American bride's honeymoon. Contrary to a cultural myth, learning the art of creative love-making takes time and practice within a secure relationship (which most premarital relationships are not).

Sexual boredom has already been mentioned and it is probably the most recurring problem for many persons in marriage. You and your mate may have experienced times when you were sexually bored. Remember that it is impossible to expect sexual interaction always to be passionate, tender, earth-shaking, and mountain-moving. But if you or your partner or the both of you together find your sex life boring over a long period of time, something may be going wrong with your relationship. Boredom is a sign that changes must be made. Boredom comes from lack of interest and involvement and may encourage escapist fantasies and affairs. But affairs and fantasies do not solve the problems; rather, they avoid them.

What feelings lie behind and underneath your boredom? Note that boredom, contrary to popular thought, is not a lack of feeling. When you say "I am bored," you have not made a passive statement; you may have expressed anger or restlessness. Are you hiding anger or resentment or hurt or other negative feelings? Dealing with boredom requires you to confront your feelings and express them to your partner. Your sex life can be deadened because your feelings that charge your sexuality have been deadened. Confront your feelings honestly and then look out for the twin allies of boredom, namely repetition and predictability. What we said on the previous point about creativity, variety, free-rein of fantasies and relinquishing trite expectations of how you are supposed to interact sexually certainly goes a long way in alleviating boredom.

Sexual dysfunctions are problems in the giving and receiving of sexual satisfaction. While some dysfunctions are physical in origin, most are psychological. Some problems are related to ignorance and naivete; others are related to fatigue and stress; others are derived from sexual inhibitions and a guilt system (leftover attitudes from childhood can be sex-spoilers); and still others from conflict within the self (conflict which may be deep and unconscious). Remember that sexual problems do not exist in a vacuum. They usually exist within the context of your marriage relationship. Both of you should seek professional counsel if you are experiencing sexual problems; some self-help books are available.

In conclusion, the sexual relationship you have established with your husband and wife should be the joyous celebration of another of loving and sharing life together in which you say to each other, "I love you ecstatically and enjoy immensely our shared life." Sex is a bonding mechanism that enhances the uniqueness of that shared life.

Prayer In Duet

Lord, help us to think of sex as you first thought of it, a gift of your grace, excellent in every way. May the times we spend in one another's arms always be treasured as precious moments to celebrate our mutual love and commitment. Invade our hearts completely and

make us sensitive with the sensitivity of Jesus our Lord, through
whom we pray. Amen.

Chapter Twenty-Five

Should Adultery Remain In Our List Of The Top Ten Sins?

In God's wisdom there was a good reason for giving his people the seventh commandment of the Decalogue.

You know that when people marry they discover that their sexual lives are quite different than they were before marriage. Their sexual activity becomes morally and socially sanctioned by society. At least this has been the traditional view. But you may feel as do many thoughtful people that in the last generation or so relationships between men and women have been changing dramatically. Have we not raised an entire generation of young men and women who do not "cleave" to a single individual *before* marriage and who balk at "cleaving" *after* marriage? The question of marital fidelity is now set in a web of cultural shifts which has accented and explored the possibilities of sexual variety through "open marriage," nonexclusive commune-style marriages, and extramarital relationships. There is a current trend to re-examine the traditional arguments for fidelity and commitment; some popular opinion-makers insist that the promise to "cleave only" should be thrown out the window with the promise to "obey." The best-selling *Open Marriage,* by John and Nena O'Neill, advocated greater sexual freedom in marriage and many listened to their argument.

How widespread is sexual infidelity? Well, there is no way to know for certain. You know that many studies and surveys have been conducted. Alfred Kinsey was the first to disclose the prevalence of extramarital intercourse back in 1948. His figures showed that 50 percent of males and 25 percent of females had experienced sex outside their marriages. The increased sexual freedom of the 1980s has raised these figures to a possible 60 percent for the males and 40 percent for females. Thus, defiance of the traditional marriage contract seems rather commonplace today, even though there are civil, religious, and emotional penalties for such violations.

Undoubtedly, you and your mate married with every intention of keeping your vow of fidelity. And even though your vows of fidelity did not explicitly state sexual exclusiveness, there was never any doubt fidelity meant sexual faithfulness first and foremost. You had heard many times the ancient commandment—"Thou shalt not commit adultery." Both Christians and nonchurched people in our society know that this prohibition is one of the Ten Commandments of the Judeo-Christian tradition. The contract to marry means giving to your partner the exclusive rights to your body and the promise that the ultimate act of intimacy is given to him/her alone. Sexual intercourse can be viewed merely as a biological act—indeed, the most pleasurable, exciting, and revealing act between two people of the opposite sex. But it is more than that. Sex as a life-uniting act is the most appropriate symbol of that commitment to a life-union. As marriage represents a sacred covenant, so sex is the seal of that covenant. The sexual act is a special kind of communication between the man and the woman who have given themselves unreservedly to one another.

Since we cannot assume that all of our readers have not and will not avoid the temptation of extramarital sex, we pose

Seven Questions To Ask Yourself *IF* You Are Having An Affair:
—How do you feel about violating your marriage vows or giving in to the temptation and pressure to "live life fully" by having an affair?

—Do you view your affair as a sin against your mate? God? your lover? your lover's mate (if married)? or do you see it as diversion and recreation?

—How is this extramarital affair affecting your emotional well-being? Is it making you a better, stronger, more loving person?

—What does your behavior tell you about your inability to maintain a committed relationship to one person? Is there anything about you that you can vow to others they can fully trust?

—Is your affair a two-way street? How would you react if your mate had an affair?

—How honest have you been with your mate? How honest have you been with your lover?

—What effect would discovery of this affair have on you? your spouse? your lover? your relatives? your Christian brothers and sisters? your work associates?

If you and your mate have been able to maintain sexual fidelity to each other, then your marriage has been blessed indeed. You may know something of the formidable commitment it is to remain sexually exclusive for the balance of a lifetime once you have made a vow. You may be disheartened to hear of sexual affairs among Christian people with whom you have long worshipped in Christian assemblies. And when you are faced with temptation you may wonder if remaining sexually faithful to your mate has all that much value when the alleged value is weighted against an intense pleasurable experience for the moment. Does the seventh commandment have as much relevance for men and women living in the latter years of the twentieth century? Is the commandment now only part of a rigid, puritanical code which does not liberate but restricts contemporary men and women? How seriously does God take adultery? Does the prohibition of adultery mean the same to us as it meant to the Jews of the Old Testament period? Could not this command be relegated to the category of ancient restrictions and practices that no longer have much meaning for us in the modern world (e.g., Old Testament views toward polygamy, intercourse during seven days of menstrual period, women as property, levirate marriage)?

In seeking answers to these questions, you might note the utter seriousness with which the Israelites viewed adultery. William Barclay comments that "it is the paradox of human nature that there was no sin regarded in Judaism with greater horror than adultery, and there was no sin which, to judge by the rebukes of the sages and prophets, was more common." Several narratives underscore the gravity with which ancient Israel viewed adultery. Joseph rebukes Potiphar's wife lest he "do this great wickedness and sin against God" (Gen. 39:9). Nathan is summoned to confront King David about his series of sins which began in lust and adultery and culminated in murder. Abimelech reacts in horror at this near escape and accused Abraham of bringing on him and his kingdom "a great sin" (Gen. 20:9). In various sections of the Old Testament, the writers link adulterers with the worst kind of sinners; additionally, the sage of the Proverbs warns the young man about the wiles of the "strange woman whose path leads to destruction" (Prov. 5:1).

The seriousness of adultery is everywhere assumed on the pages of the New Testament. Jesus in no way diminished the force of this command—indeed, he deepened its meaning so that the attitude of one's heart becomes as important as his/her physical action. Additionally, Jesus removed the double standard on adultery in order to protect women and safeguard marriage. And also in the New Testament we find the various authors linking adulterers with the worst kind of sinners. The Apostle Paul seems to say that when a man consorts with a prostitute he has committed a sin quite unlike any other sin (I Cor. 6:16-20).

At the deepest level of ethics, adultery is not related to the mere physical union of a man and a woman. This sin is related to vows and to trust. As we have noted already in this book, men and women are the only creatures God made who are capable of making vows, maintaining vows and breaking vows. Vows are commitments freely made binding free people to one another. And adultery is a special form of cheating which violates the rules by which partners agree to live their lives. As a result, adultery is a crisis of commitment. And, of course, the decision to be unfaithful means that an important segment of life must be kept secret from the mate and the world and the secrecy is quite often maintained by deception. The unfaithful partner who pretends that by keeping his adultery a secret that he/she is protecting his/her mate and safeguarding their marriage is practicing the deepest deception of all: self-deceit. You see, there are probably more rationalizations for infidelity than almost any other kind of interpersonal behavior. The breaking of faith is something that cannot be done lightly or comfortably. Also, the sexually unfaithful husband/wife must devote time and physical and emotional energy and, in some cases money, to the other man/woman. Whatever is given to the third party, in effect, is usually taken from his/her mate.

Much of this analysis is sensible to you because you are Christians. In fact, non-Christians would not accept many of the ethical principles and the Biblical basis for your decisions. For that reason, adultery in Christian marriages is particularly painful. One of the most depressing aspects of church ministry can be listening to the sad anguish of otherwise disciplined Christian men and women who allowed themselves to become entangled in a tortuous web of adulterous affairs—people who saw the circle of hurt and suffering extend to many others before they learned that this commandment was intended to serve their best interests.

Adultery can be such a devastating emotional wound to marriage that Jesus permitted it to be the only reason spouses may sever their marriage relationship. But adultery in and of itself is not able to destroy a marriage. Obviously, adultery is a terrible wound for a relationship to suffer. It mocks the contract to which the partners consented at the beginning of their marriage. It may lead to distrust, resentment, revenge, depression and other negative feelings which must be faced openly. It may render memories of the past always to be mixed with pain. It may make a reasonably good marriage much harder to sustain. But adultery as such does not have the power to terminate a life-union. Given a measure of God's grace and mercy felt in the heart of the offended person, and given a genuine love and commitment between the two mates, the marriage can be healed and made healthy. Marriage is what people make it.

Can an extramarital affair ever be a mature form of behavior? As a Christian you would not answer this question in the affirmative. But it is interesting that a number of non-Christian psychiatrists and psychoanalysts have also answered this question in the same way. In conclusion, I share some quotations from other sources on this subject.

"From my quarter-century of counseling on marital problems, I cannot recall a single case where infidelity has strengthened the marital bond." (Psychiatrist A. Stone)

"If a man has a reasonably healthy personality, is attracted to you, loves you, and has committed himself to you, you have a right to expect him to be faithful, just as he expects you to be." (Psychiatrist M. Bartusis)

"Infidelity, like alcoholism or drug addiction, is an expression of a deep basic disorder of character." (Psychologist A. Ellis)

"Infidelity is often a neurotic and sometimes psychotic pursuit of exactly the man or woman one imagines one needs. . . . It is primarily a return to behavior characteristic of adolescence or earlier." (Psychiatrist L. Saul)

"Nothing proves more conclusively the unconscious neurotic substructure of infidelity than the "arguments" of people caught in such a conflict." (Psychiatrist E. Bergler)

"On the basis of my own observation and research, I am firmly of the opinion that an extramarital affair is *never* a healthy or mature act. If a man or woman can be dependent on someone without wishing for a merger, can accept frustration without feeling sadistic or masochistic, can enjoy sex without being bombarded with competitive or incestuous fantasies, can admire a partner without overidealizing, and can be autonomous without resentment, he or she is a relatively happy human being." (Psychoanalyst Herbert S. Strean)

"Infidelity is a very chancy and unreliable means to use in searching for one's identity, in exploring one's true emotions, in struggling not only to find out what one's deepest feelings and beliefs and responses may be, but also communicating them to someone else. This is true for many reasons, including the fact that a man and a woman who are involved in an affair generally have different investments in their relationship, and these affairs are most often conducted under less than encouraging conditions. In addition, social attitudes—including those internalized by the man and woman—make it certain that in a good number of cases, the individuals will have to cope with feelings of guilt, one way or another. Either the guilt will intrude on their ability to accomplish their goals—to discover dimensions of their own personality—or it will require them to deny that the feelings exist, and in doing so, to sweep other feelings under the rug along with the discomfort of guilt.'' (Sex Researcher V. Johnson)

Prayer In Duet

Dear God, may we think of our intimate life together as a secluded walled garden where no one else is ever invited—a little private kingdom, apart from the rush and roar of the world's life, in which we can enjoy the full and free expression of our mutual love and be refreshed and renewed. Give us your strength, O God, to keep us faithful to the vows we made to each other and to you when we stood together at the altar. Day by day, following your will and trusting your strength, we make this request through Christ. Amen.

Chapter Twenty-Six

Why Did He/She Do It?

The Bible does not provide us with a listing of all the reasons why people get involved in extramarital sexual affairs, so we will attempt to formulate our own list.

The Bible provides several narratives of men and women ensnared in extramarital affairs. Undoubtedly the best known of these is the story of David and Bathsheba. You would likely say that the major factor in David's adultery was the lustful passion which he allowed to be aroused and gratified. Is David and Bathsheba's affair typical of most others? The simple way to see adultery is to dismiss it as lust, permissiveness, and degeneration. There is truth to this, of course, but it does not help for us to make sweeping generalizations. What other factors may have been operative in the lives of David and Bathsheba that contributed to this sinful liaison? Could David have neglected his spiritual life to the point that he was vulnerable? And what was Bathsheba's attitude from the time David called for her? Did she have special ego needs that were neglected by Uriah her husband? Was she so dazzled by the interest of the King that she lost all sense of moral direction?

These questions are interesting but we have no answers because the Bible does not give us much about the inner dynamics of the adulterous affairs it reports. The reasons for adultery are as many as there are adulterers and each affair has its own uniqueness and dynamics. In most affairs several important factors come into play; more than sex is usually involved. Some of the factors are external to the two involved and others relate directly to the personality and character of both people.

Jesus proclaims the will of God for marriage but does not distinguish between adulterous affairs. Yet not all adultery is the same and if we are rendering judgment it is important that we try to understand the reasons that people seek out or drift into this behavior. It is one thing to be "overtaken in a fault" in the face of a powerful temptation on a single occasion; it is quite another to decide to make a career out of carnal conquests. One man may lapse on a single occasion of temptation that emerges from a deep, long, and caring relationship with another woman. Another may avoid depth relating with any person and spend most of his adult years playing the stud who hops from one bed to another in a series of "one-night stands." The behavior of each is adultery. But they are quite different in terms of what their actions do to a marriage and what they reveal about the character of each.

We could probably list one hundred different factors which contribute to extramarital sex, but we will list ten of the most common reasons:

1. Hedonism And The Permissive Atmosphere

Our society places a premium on sensuality and sexual fulfillment and the entertainment media convince many people that there is no personal fulfillment without sexual fulfillment. Many married people who otherwise would be content are asking if they might be missing out on some real excitement in life. Some people may have extramarital sexual intimacy simply because new sexual relationships are pleasurable and exciting and moral restrictions are not meaningful to them.

2. Sexual Convenience

Married men and women find many opportunities to meet and interact with other highly interesting married men and women. With women having entered the business and professional world to assume positions once held only by males, men and women meet on a free and equal basis. Additionally, people are affluent and mobile with leisure time to be arranged.

3. Boredom And Variety Of Sexual Experience

In some marriages, not only the sexual relationship but also the entire lifestyle of the family seems to have become routinized and boring. These people suffer from a chronic "too muchness" and feel a need for deliverance not only from boredom, but from unhappiness, alienation, and a frenetic, pressured lifestyle. The idea of a new partner suggests the different, new, and exciting. In others, a man/woman may feel that his/her marriage partner is inadequate in meeting sexual needs and, consequently, seek out a person believed to be a superior sexual partner.

4. Anger And Retaliation

Anger is a strong emotion that drives people to extreme behavior. Anger and resentment can push a person toward having an affair with another in order to retaliate against a spouse for his/her infidelity or other failures. The reaction may be, "If he can, so can I." The rationalization includes the need to "get even" or "settle the score" in the most devastating way. Such a person is not really falling in love with another person but is falling in anger against his/her spouse. Sometimes the affair is an "acting-out behavior"—an expression of unconscious emotional conflict in actions rather than words. The affair is an unconscious expression of unresolved significant conflict in the marriage; it is a substitute for verbal communication.

5. Rebellion

Some feel that the monogamous nature of Christian marriage is equivalent to a modern day chastity belt and, through extramarital sex, show their independence. This rebellion may be directed against the mate who allegedly restricts freedom or against social and religious codes.

6. New Emotional Satisfaction

Many people obviously do not feel that their personal ego needs are being met in their marriage relationships and this leads some to seek satisfaction from a partner outside of marriage. It may well be that the major precipitating factor of an affair is not the feeling of sexual need but feeling the need to be appreciated. And the most common rationale or motivation given is the oft-repeated statement that "my wife/husband takes me for granted." Perhaps the second most common reason for an affair is the boost that it seems to give to self-esteem. To people who have been starved for "strokes" from each other, it might seem like a wonderful feeling to receive them from a secret lover. It is relatively easy for either a man or a woman to feel emotionally deprived in a marriage. Affairs, like the courtship before a marriage, thrive because both partners are generally quite comfortable massaging each other's egos regularly. Affair lovers spend hours telling each other how wonderful, how special, how loving and how understanding each is to the other.

7. Self Hatred And Perfectionism

People who have a severely low self-esteem but dare not reveal their blemishes within the marriage may look to someone else who does not know him/her and will not make a harsh judgment for their failures. The perfectionist may demand the ideal situation in marriage and when it is not found, then he/she seeks it in enacted fantasy.

8. Development From Friendship

An extramarital sexual affair may be the culmination of a long period in which two people of the opposite sex developed a deepening friendship based on genuine love and concern. At the front end of their relationship, sexual intercourse may have been far removed from their thinking, but the more they spent time together sharing and meeting deep needs the more their resistance weakened.

9. Sexual Deprivation

A person may be married to a sexually inactive husband/wife or one that lacks the spirit and playfulness of an interesting sexual partnership. This person may feel compelled to leave the fences of marriage in order to discover or reawaken aspects of sexuality that have been submerged or thwarted in the marriage.

10. The Aging Factor

Our society conditions people to treasure their gift of sexual attractiveness and as they grow older they sense that the aging process diminishes that all-important sex appeal. For example, an aging woman who values attractiveness can become vulnerable to any man who can convince her that she is still attractive to a lover. The highest rate of extramarital sex for women occurs in the age group 35 to 40, an age at which women may wish to prove themselves to be still desirable.

This is only a list of some of the major reasons that adults become involved in extramarital affairs. None of them, of course, is justification for adultery. When several reasons converge to exert pressure on an individual, the temptation could be powerful indeed. As Christians we believe that we have the help of God at our disposal to conquer temptation and in faith we derive strength from the statement of Paul in I Corinthians: "No temptation has seized you except what is common to man. And God is faithful; he will not let you be tempted beyond what you can bear. But when you are tempted, he will also provide a way out so that you can stand up under it" (10:13). There are many people who feel the pressures of sexual temptation and do not cross the boundaries of marital exclusiveness. Undoubtedly, many of them are timid and many lack the "safe" opportunity; on the other hand, many of them have cultivated a godly wisdom and a moral strength to safeguard them against abuse of a precious God-given gift.

Considerable research has been conducted in the field of extramarital affairs. You might be interested in a brief summary of some of the research findings; if the findings seem to be somewhat contradictory, consider them in light of gender and age differences.

—The majority of extramarital sexual involvements are sporadic. Most people involved in such relationships probably do not have extramarital sexual intercourse more than five times a year.

—Most extramarital sex does not take place as a part of an intense, long-lasting love affair but is generally self-contained and more sexual than emotional.

—Men tend to have extramarital sex when they are younger; women tend to have it when they are older.

—Women tend to describe their extramarital affairs in emotional terms while men describe theirs in more sexual ones. For women extramarital sex tends not to be an isolated event but clearly implies a willingness to maintain a series of emotional experiences with the sexual partner.

—Two important variables appear to be related to extramarital affairs: happiness of the marriage and/or premarital sexual permissiveness. In happy marriages there is less likelihood that a partner will seek outside sexual relationships. And persons who break the religious and social prohibitions against premarital sex are less likely to be restrained by prohibitions against extramarital sex.

—Sex without love seems to be less acceptable and less enjoyable to both men and women than was the case several years ago (see survey in *Psychology Today,* July, 1983).

—People without strong religious commitment are twice as likely to be involved in extramarital affairs than people with strong religious commitment.

Prayer

Dear God, I want to know myself as you know me. By your enabling grace, give me the courage to be transparent and the strength to make it possible. Help me to be honest with you, with myself, and with the significant others in my life. Through Jesus. Amen.

Chapter Twenty-Seven

Your Mate Has Been Unfaithful—Now What?

From both the Bible and from good judgment we may draw some guidelines for the healing of a broken marriage.

Most marriages that have continued a number of years have adjusted to births and deaths, illness and financial difficulty, the challenges of parenting, the pains of overwhelming commitment and unwelcome relocations. Yet they have bobbed up and down like a cork on choppy waters. But the deadliest crisis is the crisis of trust between you and your mate. What if your partner has been unfaithful to you? What if you have discovered that he/she has been involved in an extramarital affair? How do you respond? How should you react in this kind of situation? Does your Christian commitment have any bearing on your response?

Perhaps this chapter does not seem relevant to your situation. The Christian marriage must have deeper insight and greater resources that render it less likely to face an adulterous situation than a marriage of nonbelievers. But the fact is, just as the rate of extramarital affairs is increasing in society, this permissiveness spills over and affects Christian marriages. And most of us would feel that at times we have had to cope with "smaller" infidelities, such as with lying, unkept promises, with attacks, with feelings of betrayal.

Unfaithfulness can be a special kind of crisis situation for you and all other married people for two reasons. First, an adulterous affair affects the emotions differently from any other event in your marriage and it is almost impossible for you to remain objective in the face of what has been revealed. If you are in this situation, no one is expecting you to remain cool and detached as you try to work through this crisis. After infidelity, a couple's relationship and thinking always change. Second, in every other kind of crisis your marriage faces you can draw on each other's strength. But in the crisis of trust you have only your depleted inner resources to fall back on; as a Christian, thankfully, you have your faith in God and hopefully the support of Christian friends to bolster those inner resources. Yet nothing is more discouraging than to invest depleted energy and dwindling morale in a sincere effort to heal a relationship and then seeing little or nothing change for the better. Often the failure is due to ignorance of what the Bible teaches about reconciliation and of the principles that lead to healing and enrichment of human relationships.

Let's imagine that you have discovered that your husband/wife is involved in an extramarital affair. What are some ways in which you could respond? The following responses are both typical and understandable, but to respond in any of these ways would be detrimental to your relationship:

—You could denounce and condemn your mate. You could angrily remind your mate that he/she has broken both a law of God and a vow of marriage. Such condemnation is not likely to be effective; indeed, your mate may have already engaged in self-condemnation, especially if low self-esteem was a major factor in the infidelity.

—You could become violent in this already volatile situation. Your disgust and frustration may make you want to dash your best china to the floor or hit your mate over the head with a bat. Your anger is natural, of course, but violent words or action may only serve as a catalyst for retaliation by your mate. And if anger continues with no positive overtones of understanding and forgiveness, the unfaithful mate finds greater justification for what he/she has done.

—You could tell every person you know, especially those people who have confidence in your mate, that he/she has been unfaithful and that he/she is a bad person. Such reporting might be a way of compensating for your hurt, but it is a way of seeking revenge that will return to haunt your marriage. Certainly you will need to vent your feelings with a third party but be selective about your confidants on such a private matter.

—You could issue threats and ultimatums, such as "I'll get you for this" or "If you ever see that person again I'll . . ." Vindictive comments flow so easily when your ego has been shattered, but threats and warnings will push your mate further away from you. Remember that your marriage may have been on shaky ground prior to his/her affair and has moved to crumbling ground once the affair has surfaced. What you do and say next is vitally important to the survival of the relationship.

—You could ask your mate's family, closest friend, or your minister to talk to him/her and "straighten him/her out." This kind of unilateral rescue operation is not likely to be appreciated.

—You could go see the other party involved just to see what he/she looks like, to plead with that person, or to verbally or physically attack him/her. Such action is likely to give temporary relief and permanent regret.

—You could ask for minute details of your mate's romantic involvement. Knowing about the sordid side of the affair may satisfy curiosity but the questions you really want to ask (egs. "Did the two of you make love in this house?" "What was she like in bed?") are questions that your mate will not want to answer and can only produce further hurt and emotional distance.

—You could try to answer the question "Who is to blame?" Here you are trying to be more objective, but "blame" is a loaded word. Even if the blame can be proved, the real reasons probably lie with both of you and getting bogged down in affixing blame only delays reconciliation. Reciprocal finger-pointing is not going to resolve the problem.

These natural and typical responses are hardly calculated to save your marriage. Let's assume that there is much about your marriage that makes it worth saving. Let's assume you are wise enough to realize that contentment is not gained by tearing apart the past. Let's assume also that because you are Christians you take your marriage commitment seriously. You know that while Jesus decreed that divorce is only permissible if it is for the cause of adultery, he did not command that adultery must terminate the marriage relationship. The New Testament places high value on honoring commitments, healing brokenness, and reconciling interpersonal differences. Let's reverse some of the above typical responses in order to approach your problem in a way that will most likely bring healing and reconciliation.

1. Try not to be hostile or vindictive. Anger can be owned and expressed in clear statements rather than by contempt, humiliation, sarcasm, or namecalling.

2. Avoid questioning why this affair happened, at least in the beginning. There will be time enough to sort out all the casual factors at a later date. Don't ever push too hard. People communicate only when they are ready and when they trust you sufficiently.

3. Own up to your feelings. Don't blame your feelings on someone else ("You infuriate me!" or "You've broken up this whole family!"). This is avoiding the responsibility for what you feel and is a concession that someone else has control of your emotional life.

4. Never assume you know how your mate is feeling. Simply ask your mate. Faulty assumptions can prevent reconciliation. For example, you may assume your partner to be madly in love with the other man/woman and that may not be true at all. The affair may have been triggered by a feeling of loneliness or inadequacy and a strong

temptation from someone for whom he/she did not really care.

5. Do not make a hasty decision to terminate the marriage. Big decisions need to be made in the context of many factors that cannot be processed instantly. Reflect on the possibilities and consequences of each choice you could make. Each of you should listen to the views of the other. Actually, this is a time of negotiation—of making allowances for the needs, values, and preferences of the other. Negotiation is a process between equals and the process does not work when there is interruption, refusal to listen, childish tantrums, ultimatums, and ridicule. If you allow no alternative to dissolving the marriage, negotiation is at an end.

6. Seek qualified help. You and your partner should seek help together but you can seek help even if your mate is unwilling. Unfortunately, many people have the feeling that turning to others to help them solve personal problems is a sign of weakness. And making that call to a psychologist, psychiatrist, family counselor, or minister may be one of the most difficult things you have ever felt compelled to do. But you are truly a strong person, not a weak one, when you ask for help. Ultimately, you do not go to a people-helper because your spouse is having or has had an affair, but you go because there is a need and conflict within you that needs to be resolved.

7. Forgive your partner's sin. This is the crucial issue and we have saved it for last in this listing. And yet forgiveness is the most important action of all. There are plenty of occasions in every marriage that call for forgiveness. Part of our humanness is that we hurt the most readily and the most deeply the people we love the most. Perhaps this is because there are so many hopes and expectations developed between people in loving relationships. Forgiving is the greatest way in which you are loving. Forgiveness is an unconditional gift of your love. When you and your mate come to realize that in complex difficulties involving sin and failure that it is impossible to fix blame or assess shares of guilt, and when you realize a common need for continual compassion from God and from others, you have developed a basis for extending forgiving love to one another.

Let's summarize seven important points about forgiveness that are drawn from Christian ethics:

—Forgiveness is possible. Adultery is not the unpardonable sin. Every sin that is confessed can be forgiven.

—Forgiveness is not basically a feeling. It is an act of the will bringing restoration. Of course, the experience of forgiveness must eventually be deeply felt, but you must choose to forgive even when all your feelings cry out against it.

—Forgiveness is not pretending or forgetting. You cannot ignore the fact that an event has occurred. Forgiveness is not an eraser that wipes the memory of the act forever from your mind. There is a difference between remembering a deed and treating a mate as through the sin was not committed.

—Forgiveness is not the same as tolerance or leniency. You tolerate or are lenient toward an evil deed only when there is moral apathy. Forgiveness in no way diminishes the gravity of the offense.

—Forgiveness does not demand guarantees. "I'll forgive you if you promise me that you will never be unfaithful again!" is conditional love and conditional forgiveness. Christian forgiveness is always a venture and a risk.

—Forgiveness has nothing to do with justice. If you are determined to stand on your "rights" in marriage, it is not likely you will forgive. As a Christian, you must allow justice to give way to mercy. Tender love and mercy restore, reconcile, and heal. The ultimatum "I forgive you this time but I won't forgive you again" misses the spirit of Christ-like forgiveness.

Forgiveness is a reciprocal process. Your forgiveness should provoke your mate to forgive you and vice versa. Forgiveness is never a "paid-up policy"—it requires continual investment. The New Testament enjoins us to confess our sins to each other and pray for each other (James 5:16). The three most important words in marital communication may be "I love you," but almost every day there can be a need for love to be expressed in the next three most important words, "I'm sorry, dear." How much do you feel the grace of God in your own lives? Do you not feel that if God has forgiven you of a great deal that you can forgive each other? Do you feel that God gives you the resources to keep your marriage together and growing no matter what crisis it encounters?

Scripture And Prayer In Duet

Get rid of all bitterness, rage and anger, brawling and slander, along with every form of malice. Be kind and compassionate to one another, forgiving each other, just as in Christ God forgave you.

(Eph. 4:31-32)

"Dear God, may each new day bring us the peace and fulfillment that comes from being deeply committed to the sanctity of another human being—and to our marriage. Through Jesus, Amen."

Chapter Twenty-Eight

Are Adultery And Infidelity Synonymous?

If Biblical principles guide our thinking and conduct, we discover that fidelity is a larger concept than we might want to admit.

Perhaps you have thought of your major task in living out your marital commitment as maintaining fidelity. We have spoken of Christian marriage as an intimate relationship characterized by total and exclusive commitment. The relationship is continuous, lifelong, and growing. Marriage was not given just for the control of sex, but for the liberation and fulfillment of personhood. Thus, if we speak positively and optimistically about marriage, we must also speak affirmatively about fidelity.

How do you think of fidelity? You would certainly say that fidelity has something to do with the sexual exclusiveness of your marriage relationship. Your sexual life is a nonnegotiable item of your marriage ethic. But do you think of marital fidelity as a fence or a wall to keep you away from "forbidden fruit"? Do you see fidelity as relating to non-sexual aspects of your relationship with your mate? Is fidelity nothing more than putting a leash on sexual lust? Is the richness of the concept of fidelity captured in the prohibition "Thou shalt not commit adultery"?

Let's begin to think of fidelity as something far larger than our sexuality. As Lewis Smedes puts it rather bluntly in *Sex for Christians,* "Fidelity certainly involves the location of one's genitals, but it also stretches far beyond; it extends into the whole marital relationship." The moral shortsightedness of many Christians is evident when we see Christian morality in negative terms—what we must not think and what we must not do. Many of us have insisted in legalistic fashion that marriage is for life, divorce is wrong, and that infidelity if not to be tolerated. But at the same time it is possible that many of us have made little effort to work at our marriages, to improve our relationships with our partners, to dedicate ourselves to a life of creative ministry for the well-being of our partners, and to keep our love alive and deepening through all the changes, difficulties and milestones of shared existence. As a result there is no experiencing of the vitality and exuberance that are intended to accompany Christian marriage. Whether sharing meal times or leisure times, even a Christian couple can look idly about, in bored resignation, rarely taking notice of the presence of the other except to pass the salt or change the channel. Such a lifestyle is a vivid illustration that "the written code kills, but the Spirit gives life" (2 Cor. 3:6). It is quite likely that no law, either civil or religious, ever held a marriage together in any kind of rich and fulfilling fashion.

We should make clear that we are not minimizing the importance of negative fidelity. Neither are we saying that there should be no law with respect to marriage. As in every area of human behavior, the law in marriage serves as a check on sin. There is law in Christian ethics and we should be grateful for it. Your early indoctrination in law may well have prevented you from some foolish deeds that you undoubtedly would have deeply regretted later. Certainly the commandment proscribing adultery has prevented some sexual infidelity and, as a result, some couples have been held together who would otherwise have separated. But law is negative. Law can prevent evil; it has limited power to create.

How many men and women have you heard assert that they have lived up to the ideal of Christian fidelity in their marriages because they never once strayed from the marital bed? Yet, honoring the ideal of fidelity is not based on keeping codes and legalistic "contracts" alone. A married person can be too busy, too preoccupied, too tired, too uninterested, too timid or simply too callous and indifferent and therefore unappealing to others, or too fearful, to be seriously tempted to commit adultery. He/she may be able to say that he/she never strayed or never cheated; but he/she may not be able to claim honestly that he/she was fully devoted to the growth of the partner, that the partner is the most important person in his/her life and that the partner will always be at the center of his/her heart and be treated and respected as such.

What we are saying is that fidelity must be based on what you are and what you do as much as on what you are not and what you do not do. You and your mate could be faithful to your vow of sexual exclusiveness without ever making your marriage the kind of personal union that God had in mind when he spoke of two people becoming "one flesh." Currently, I work as pulpit minister for the Otter Creek church. If I am faithful as a hired servant of this church, it will not be because I do not spend my time ministering to the Hillsboro church or to the Ashwood church—it is because of the positive ministering to the body of people which engages me. Fidelity is a moral achievement when it is person and relationship-directed; it is less moral when it is function-based. There are many negative reasons for a kind of functional fidelity (we have already cited some). But, at the core, as Smedes points out, "fidelity in partnership is commitment to an ongoing, dynamic, changing, sensitive facing off of two people bent on the total well-being of each other. And each is faithful to the extent that he is dedicated to the constant growth, healing, and regrowth of the other person. Fidelity, in short, is person-oriented."

The Bible gives us a model of fidelity—God and his people. This model is especially clear in Old Testament history. God chose Israel to be his special people and bound himself to this people by covenant. God blessed his people by giving them direction for their lives and strength for their tasks. In return God asked for Israel's fidelity and love to him as the only God. In the enacted parable of Hosea we have a depiction both of God's fidelity to his people and the infidelity of his people. Hosea takes a prostitute, Gomer, for a wife and the three children of that union are given prophetic names of Jezreel, Not Pitied, and Not My People in token of God's judgment on Israel. In spite of the marriage and the children, Gomer continues in her adulterous ways, eventually forsaking Hosea and falling into slavery. At God's command Hosea does not cease to love her in spite of her infidelity, her shameless lifestyle, and the despicable condition to which she lowered herself. In expression of undying love, Hosea buys back his slave-wife and pledges her to new fidelity (Hosea 1-3: 3).

The story of Hosea needs little exposition. God gives evidence of his fidelity by always loving his people, even when they are unfaithful, and always taking positive and patient steps to win his people back into the course of healthy and growing relationship. God's enduring love always sought the good of Israel. In our age God has the same kind of steadfast love and fidelity for the church. As a married couple you can look at this divine model and capture some of the sense of what positive fidelity is all about—it is creative, dynamic, enduring, loyal, and person-oriented. Does this describe the kind of fidelity to which you and your partner are pledged?

Prayer

Dear God, thank you for your model of positive and dynamic fidelity toward people who covenant themselves to you and thank you for your grace and direction that make some measure of that fidelity possible in my marriage. Through Jesus, Amen.

Chapter Twenty-Nine

How Important Are Spiritual Growth And Spiritual Unity In Our Marriage?

Here's some straight talk about what may be the most important topic raised in this book.

On Sunday evening, November 20, 1983, some 100 million Americans gathered around their television sets to watch the ABC special movie "The Day After," a film depicting the impact on a local community of a successful nuclear attack. You may recall the controversy that surrounded the film and how some labeled it propaganda before it was aired. Regardless of the political implications of the film, great interest in it, particularly by the school children, was evident. Some teenagers were profoundly affected by the apocalyptic vision of mass destruction. How do you handle the thought that your house, your family, and the world you know may be destroyed? The answer, of course, is that the best way to handle the destruction of this planet is to make certain you have a better place to go when this earthly system no longer exists.

You may be wondering how this relates to your marriage. You know that it is your religious faith and values that enable you to cope with the major passages and the crises of life. Faith enables you to understand and interpret what otherwise could be tragic and incomprehensible. And it may well be that the primary and most important source for the birth and nurturance of religious faith is within the home and family relationships. We tend to think of the church as an institution and we are justified in doing so. But the real continuing life of the church is made possible only because it is a fellowship of Christian families—families which generate a spirit of loyalty and devotion to Christ and transmit that spirit to their children, enabling the transition of faith from one generation to another. Is faith in God being developed in your home? How important are religious values at your house? Is there spiritual intimacy in your marriage relationship? Are the two of you growing spiritually? Do you have a faith that outlives this earthly system?

Perhaps we are now ready to make the most important point yet to be made in this book: Growth in horizontal, person-to-person relationships and growth on the vertical or spiritual plane complement and reinforce each other, and no single factor does more to give a marriage joy or keep it a venture in mutual fulfillment than a shared commitment to God and spiritual values. The moments when both of you can feel the presence of God and his Spirit in your lives are those moments of sharing which are the most tender and precious in your relationship.

In a discussion of intimacy in marriage, Howard Clinebell states that intimacy with God and intimacy with human beings are interrelated. The times that you feel emotionally isolated from other human beings are the times that you most likely feel like a spiritual orphan in the universe, regardless of whatever your head-level religious convictions may be. On the other hand, when you feel a strong bond with all other humans you usually have a sense of connection with nature and with Divine Presence, whether or not it is expressed in traditional religious forms. "The ability to establish, nurture, and sustain an intimate human relationship, and the ability to commune vitally with nature, the universe, and God, are closely related," Clinebell points out. "Furthermore, each of these kinds of relatedness profoundly influences the other. He who loves his spouse, whom he has seen, is better able to love God, whom he has not seen, and vice versa."

The area of trust provides a clear illustration of this relatedness between spiritual intimacy and interpersonal intimacy. What does it mean to be able to form a human relationship of mutual trust? Does it not mean that you find the "significant other" in that relationship to be dependable and consistent? Wouldn't it be a relationship in which the two of you felt free to be yourselves, free to adventure and to discover, fully accepted, and no longer needing to do things to prove your worth? This kind of human liberation is felt by the fresh breeze of grace flowing through the stifling atmosphere of legalism and moralism. If you know this reality in your marriage then you are much better equipped to experience it in other relationships. If you have a source of regular trust renewal in your spiritual life, you have a steady foundation for trustful human relationships. And your trust in God and his fidelity to the community of faith and to you as an individual gives you the strength you need to be faithful and trusting toward others during periods of difficulty and stress.

Isn't it interesting that the family is God's great metaphor for his special community of people, the church? The imagery of the family is locked into Scripture from the call of Abraham onward. One reason that God created the family was for the purpose of making it the central carrier of the godly value system. Other institutions of this world—corporations, government bureaucracies, the military, schools—are based on competition and status. You rise in them by demonstrating greater worth or by out-performing the competition.

Against this background, God provides the blueprint for a social unit called the family, a haven from the rest of the world where worth is determined only by mere chance of birth. The son with special needs has as much worth as the Merit scholarship winner; his acceptance in the family is not questioned. The prodigal boy who squanders the inheritance from his father is welcomed as enthusiastically at the dinner table as the older son who followed all the rules.

The New Testament teaches that we Christians are in the family of God. God is our father. Jesus proclaimed that God would adopt us as sons, not as slaves. We inherit the privileges of sonship. Jesus, in one sense, is our older brother (cf. Heb. 2:11 and Mark 3:31-34) and we are joint-heirs with him. We are accepted and loved and forgiven because we are sons and daughters of our heavenly Father.

What does this have to do with your marriage? Everything. The unconditional love and acceptance that God has for his people serve as a model for all of our marriages. You may act in such a way as to move beyond God's approval and his rewards, but you can never travel beyond the sphere of God's love and solicitous concern. Conversely, when you and your lifetime partner approximate ideal love, you have experienced the closest thing on earth to divine love. Your marriage and your family ties are the only relationships which could, by any stretch of the imagination, be called "heaven on earth." But these relationships carry with them the potential of creating "hell on earth." You certainly know of the human tendency of change and manipulate what you do not like. Most of us at one time or another have wanted to control the other person, squeezing him/her into our mold and personality. By contrast, God valued freedom so much that he built into every person the capacity to reject him.

The choice between heaven or hell may begin in our marriage and family relationships. Your marriage is crucially important because it allows you a frontier to practice God's value system, so that you may derive strength to introduce that system to people who do not really know Jesus Christ. The fact that there is strife and conflict in your marriage does not mean that God cannot mediate his love to you through this special relationship. In Christian marriage all of us are tiptoeing through a field of land mines on the way to paradise. Dostoevski once declared, "I ponder, 'what is hell?' I maintain it is the suffering of being unable to love." If true, then what is heaven? Do you not have the best insight into heaven when the two of you become spiritually and then physically and emotionally one?

Now let's deal with a problem frequently found in marriages: what do you do when your mate seemingly has no religious faith or commitment and who may even be antagonistic to your own spiritual devotion? If you find yourself in this kind of situation you know how difficult life can become and how profoundly this type of conflict influences your children. A related problem arises when the husband and wife come from different denominational backgrounds and each insists on being loyal to his/her own religious heritage. In this situation it is very important for the two of you to search for and discover a core of shared meanings which transcend your differences and give you a basis for spiritual intimacy. The discovery may entail some kind of compromise in shared religious exercises. That kind of search is a tough struggle, but the resulting enrichment is well worth the effort. When married couples cannot share openly in faith experiences and when they cannot worship together, they not only deny themselves one of life's most satisfying experiences but they also present their older children with a dilemma. Couples who can be completely united about religious faith and church loyalty generally find they can reach unity about all other important issues.

Among the women who are reading these pages there may be some "church widows" who would earnestly seek to change that status. These remarks are addressed to you women. You may have seen the Norman Rockwell painting of a Sunday home scene depicting an immaculately dressed mom and well-scrubbed kids marching past a pajama-clad dad who slinks down in his easy chair with his Sunday paper; the father has that kind of temporarily-embarrassed-look about not joining his family on the way to church assemblies. If that is similar to the way it is at your house, these suggestions are for you:

1. Make sure that religious conflict in your marriage is not simply a cover for other kinds of conflict between the two of you. What may appear on the surface as a "religious problem" may be a long-standing, repressed problem, such as a dominance-submission struggle.

2. Check your attitude. Christianity may seem to cause resentment in your husband if you come across to him and others as feeling superior. Is your faith a mature one? The mature believer rejects all attempts to justify herself and try to be perfect. She realizes that the main difference between her and the unbeliever is that the

Christian knows she needs help and has freely admitted it to God. Also, the mature believer has learned to say not only "My God for me" but also "I for my God." She knows that she does not have to be perfect for God to use her.

If your husband was raised in another religious tradition, be on guard against religious one-up-man-ship, a "game" based on exclusivism in your religious tradition (*ie.,* that your tradition is the only right, true, Christian church and is "obviously superior"). This self-righteous attitude creates conflict by putting your husband's tradition "one-down."

3. Check your messages to your husband when the two of you discuss religion. If he does not seem to be as interested in religion as you would like, try approaching him with serious dialogue about the meaning of human existence and the nature of eternal destiny. Beating him over the head with notions of "duty" or laying on guilt trips ("what will people think?") may only serve to confirm his views about the pettiness and hypocrisy of many practicing religious folks.

4. Don't nag. Nagging is reminding him of something he already knows. It is completely ineffective.

5. Pray for your husband privately but persistently. Pray for wisdom, understanding, strength, and, most of all, patience.

6. Most important, always remember the advice of Peter to Christian women married to unbelievers in the first century. The New Testament strategy for converting your husband is not verbal communication but by lifestyle evangelism (cf. I Pet. 3:1-6). Allow your husband to be persuaded by your Christ-like behavior and attitudes rather than trying to persuade him by verbal arguments and eloquence. Few men will allow themselves to be pushed on matters of religion, but when your man sees you are being refreshed by your faith and devotion he will want to drink from the same well.

Of coures the advice given here to women can be applied as easily by husbands whose wives are not Christians.

Once you and your mate begin relating to the Lord in terms of daily dependence, the relationship between the two of you will grow in depth. But how do you foster spiritual growth in a marriage between Christians? Here are some suggestions that may work for you:

1. Each of you could have a quiet time each day. This would be a time for meditation or for reading the Bible or other inspirational books.

2. Each of you could draft personal programs of study and self-growth. This would be a commitment to reading or continuing

education courses. Special times could be reserved for the sharing of new insights and ideas with each other.

3. You could pray together as husband and wife. Your prayer life could be a vital part of radical self-disclosure to your partner and God. You may find it difficult to pray with your mate, but what better prayer partner could there be than your marriage partner? You might begin by joining hands and spending moments in silent prayer. When you begin to verbalize your prayer, communicate with God conversationally and directly as though you were addressing each other. Prayer in marriage need not be like rigid prayer in worship assemblies which sometimes seems to be like prayer leaders making speeches to one another.

4. Family devotionals could be instituted in your home if they are not already. Getting everyone in the family involved in family worship will make indelible impressions for a lifetime. A goal for your family could be that everybody prays for everybody else every day, including in-laws, grandparents, house guests, perhaps even pets. A number of useful devotional guides are published for oral reading, such as *Power for Today,* if you are uncomfortable with complete spontaneity.

5. Become involved in the life and worship of a church which enables all of you to have instructive, nurturing, and trust-restoring experiences. The essential message of the Christian faith is that, while we are saved as individuals, there are no Lone Ranger-disciples; we all need the supportive fellowship and undergirding relationships of brothers and sisters of likeminded faith and we need the strength and affirmation that comes from corporate worship.

Scripture

[And Joshua said:] Now fear the Lord and serve him with all faithfulness. . . . but if serving the Lord seems undesirable to you, then choose for yourselves this day whom you will serve, whether the gods your forefathers served beyond the River, or the gods of the Amorites, in whose land you are living. But as for me and my household, we will serve the Lord.''

(Joshua 24:14-15).

Chapter Thirty

Does Marriage Get Better
With The Passing Of Time?

Marriage in the later years of your life will not be radically different for you than marriage at any stage of life, but the mellow quality of the later years carries with it the possibility of new depths of intimacy and new levels of satisfaction.

You've probably seen the television commercial where the husband reassuringly tells his aging wife: "Honey, you're not getting older—you're getting better." That's quite a compliment even though it isn't true. All of us are getting older. Maybe you don't show your age as much as most people. Maybe you are becoming a more pleasant and appealing person as you age. But you do get older. And the aging process brings its own special package of problems and circumstances that must be handled.

If you have not waved goodbye to the youngest of your children, are you preparing yourself for that time? Are you aware that when your last child leaves your nest that you will be entering one of the most critical periods of marital adjustment? Have you thought about what it might be like in your marriage after you retire from a salaried position? Do you expect your marriage to get better? How will you be spending your time? Do you foresee any personality changes in yourself during those "empty nest" years? Isn't there a difference between "growing old" and "growing up"? "Growing old" requires nothing but staying alive during the passage of time while "growing up" requires practical wisdom and discipline.

These questions are important ones because people are living longer now than they lived in previous generations. It is not at all uncommon for a couple to live some 10 or 15 years beyond the age of retirement. While no one has a lease on life, you should plan for these post-retirement years. You should be vigorous in energy and still active in organizational life and yet, by the time you are in your 60s, freed from responsibilities of job and family to do some of the activities together that you have not had time for previously. In our culture couples in their 60s are not really old yet, and few of them are ready for retirement village or convalescent living. Provided that your financial stability is secured, these years can be some of the happiest that you have ever known. These years of later marriage should be highly productive and creative times in which each of you finds new energy and new stimulation for reinvestment in new careers, new hobbies, and joint projects in which the two of you can find new meaning in life.

In many ways and places the Bible teaches us that the kind of foundation we lay or the kind of sowing we do determines how long the house stands or the quality of the harvest. That principle certainly applies to your marriage. If you have learned to communicate in some depth, and if you have learned how to spend leisure time creatively, the passing years usually increase the intimacy of your relationship. If, on the other hand, you have not enjoyed spending time together and you have done little depth sharing, you will find your marriage in later years to be even more barren than before—a kind of emotional wasteland. You may know of couples who have developed parallel lives, linking up at fewer and fewer interest points as the years go by. In some cases, this is symbolized by the two sleeping in separate bedrooms or perhaps even living in separate sections of the house. They remain married because it is too expensive or too embarrassing to separate or because they gain some neurotic satisfaction from living in the psychological ice age. What kind of patterns of interaction are being established in your marriage? Do you expect these patterns to be continued or changed during your retirement years? Have you thought about the amount of discipline required to change life-long habits?

During the later years of marriage you should come to the most mature understanding of faithfulness. Faithfulness is impossible if you cannot believe that your love has a future. Faithfulness refuses to consider your lives as a series of hastily called, disjointed masquerades; it does not rest until there is a connectedness to your lives. The only real difference between a faithful relationship and a romantic fling or passing love affair is this sense of time. Faithfulness is two people making their lives continually available to each other in order to create a common story. Certainly the most precious gift of a faithful relationship is the gift of time and availability. Most people just are not available to you most of the time. You have probably opened up many conversations with others by apologizing for taking some of their time. It seems that the less available you are, the more important you can claim to be. Jesus, of course, did not operate that way. His entire ministry can be described as a kind of faithful availability to people who rarely received such gifts. Jesus gave time to sinners, to the dispossessed, to the needy, and he refused to allow his friends to keep children from him.

A major contribution to the happiness experienced in marriage in the later years should be an acceptance of your mate as he/she actually is. By this time it will become apparent that change in personal habits and lifestyle is not going to take place. People are who they are, for better or for worse, and all the hoping in the world is not going to bring change. When such expectations of change are relinquished, the blessing of enjoying and appreciating your partner's true self is present. During this last season of marriage you will have the opportunity to establish what psychologist Erik Erikson calls "ego-integrity." Rather than wishing life could have been different, Erikson notes, you accept all that life has brought, integrate it into a personal life-history, and pronounce it to be good. It is as if in mature age you survey all that has gone before and respond with a resounding "yes!" This affirmation about the goodness of your life must be rooted in the grace and mercy of God who forgives and forgets your past sins.

As you both engage in life-review, you may conclude that marriage was not simply the best of your daydreams but at times was the worst of your nightmares. It is always hard to accept the shadow of evil and failure in the midst of deepest love, but, as John Dunne has stated, "genuine emotional ties are always ambivalent." So too, the times that married people share will always alternate between daydreams and nightmares, good times and bad, progress and failure, ups and downs, "something more" and "more than enough." Eccleisiastes reminds us that though we are permitted to consider time in its wholeness, we "cannot fathom what God has done from beginning to end" (3:11). A life-review from a Christian perspective is the best means of combatting a sense of worthlessness and despair. The Apostle Paul is quite explicit on this point: "And we know that in all things God works for the good of those who love him, who have been called according to his purpose" (Rom. 8:28).

During this season of your marriage there will likely be greater closeness between you and your adult children. Incidentally, almost all studies show that this closeness tends to be with the daughter more than with the son; women are more involved in kin affairs of all types than men. As you get older and turn to your adult children you may experience a role reversal. During the previous adult years you as parents had been responsible for your children and now your children may become responsible for you. You may find yourselves giving much less than you receive from your children. Your relationship with your children is so important to the overall fulfillment and satisfaction you will experience during these later years of marriage. Will you be able to allow your children to be the real parents of your grandchildren? Will you be able to accept sharp differences in religious values and political beliefs with your children? Will you have the grace to handle the new role of dependency on your children? Can you maintain frequent contact and affectionate relations with your children so that the obligation to help in time of need does not become the dominant element in your relationship?

You know that life in the later years can be stressful and difficult. The world changes so fast that the elderly feel a sense of loss for the way things were. Along with change is the frequent possibility that the aged will become isolated and marginal to the changing world around them. The influence of youth values affects everyone in the aging process. Both men and women are prone to periods of depression about aging, though men appear to panic less about aging than do women. The decline in energy and strength can be a problem for the male. Yet men are "allowed" to age in ways women are not and often they receive status and positive supports related to aging. For many women aging is a humiliating process of gradual sexual disqualification; the decline in physical attractiveness that accompanies aging can be a great source of conflict. Erma Bombeck may have said it best when she conceded, "I've got everything I had 25 years ago. But now it's all four inches lower."

Also, it is inevitable that suffering will be a part of later life. You know that death is inevitable and that one of you will face the specter of life without the other. How suffering and death and loneliness are faced in the later years has a great deal to say about how much meaning is found in this period of life. The Christian faith is clear about suffering and hardship; they are as much a part of life as joy and pleasure and, rather than simply enduring them in the stoic sense, should be embraced as a stimulus to growth.

Aging may present many little serendipities to you. Most likely you will find yourself in the happy role of grandparenting. Grandparents can often look at their grandchildren in a way they could not view their own children. They often can find the joy of generous giving because they have few rights or obligations. Grandparents do not have the task of bringing grandchildren up, of saying no, and of sacrificing the present to the future. Affection from your grandchildren and time spent with them could bring you boundless delight. In the later years you should also find sexual interest and capacity have not abandoned you. The research studies by Masters and Johnson make it clear that many older couples enjoy the sexual act as long as they are alive. The intensity of the passion may be diminished and the frequency of intercourse may be lessened, but the enjoyment of sexual relationship need not be impaired simply by aging. The joy of touching and caressing should always be present.

The options for how the later years of marriage are spent were never greater than they are now. Instead of emptiness, these years can be seen as years of opportunities to do the things you have always wanted to do but could not because of work obligations and financial commitments—traveling, reading, hobbies, special projects. Most important, you may find that you have much more time that you can give directly to the Lord through involvement in church ministry. Find "your thing" and get involved in the needs of others. Discover at this point in your life, if you have not already, the immeasurable joy of giving yourself away. Marriage during this season can be the most satisfying and fulfilling times of life.

"Come along, grow old with me
     The last of life for which the first was made"

(Robert Browning).

A Scripture, A Thought, And A Prayer

"Give generously, for your gifts will return to you later. Divide your gifts among many, for in the days ahead, you yourself may need much help" (Ecc. 11:1-2, *The Living Bible*).

"Time is the greatest of all human mysteries. . . . The way we respond to the challenge of time is a test of what we are, of what we are becoming. We grow older day by day. . . . Does that fact disturb us greatly, little, sometimes, often? How else are we growing in the same time? . . . For life is—or has—this unique energy possessed of sensitivity and perceptiveness that makes for itself a web of relationships, thus binding its past to its future."

—Robert MacIver

Lord, you know better than I know that
I am growing older, will some day be old.
Help me to accept this reality and may I never be afraid to look directly into those well-lit mirrors.

Help me to make the most of every day, every week, and every month that I have with my lifetime mate. By now I know how precious they are. May I fully support my partner in the adjustments to retirement. Give me the wisdom to enjoy constructively the new leisure that retirement brings.

Keep me from getting talkative and particularly from the fatal habit of thinking I must say something on every subject and every occasion.

Spare me from an ugly disposition. Make me sweeter and more sensitive to the needs of others than I have ever been before, yet release me from craving to try to straighten out everybody's business.

Make me thoughtful but not moody. Help me to prepare myself and my mate to live as a widow or widower by strengthening inner resources and outer relationships.

Keep my memories and reflections sweet and uplifting and spare me from brooding over the past mistakes you have already forgiven. Help me to keep most of those memories to myself. With my vast store of wisdom it seems a pity not to use it all, but you know, Lord, that I want a few friends at the end of life. Keep my mind free from the recital of endless details. Give me wings to get to the point.

Seal my lips on my aches and pains except for the times I talk to you in prayer. Remind me that there are precious few people who care about my medical history or want a chronology of my surgeries and medicinal prescriptions. They are increasing and my love of rehearsing them is becoming sweeter as the years go by. On the other hand, I ask for grace enough to listen to the tales of others' pains. Help me endure them patiently.

Keep me reasonably sweet. I do not ask to be a saint as the world thinks of sainthood. Remind me that a sour old person is one of the crowning works of the devil. When I am "put out" with my children's advice, like "don't forget your medicine" or "be careful walking along the road," may I remember that they counsel me only because they love me.

May I always remember that laughter is one of the best medicines around and I thank you that it is free. Lord, there may be some tough things in store for me in the next few years so help me to take you and your kingdom ethics and values with utmost seriousness and then to take everything else not quite so seriously. If I run out of things to laugh at, help me to laugh at myself.

Teach me the glorious lesson that occasionally it is possible that I may be mistaken. May I remember that as long as I have a sound mind, with or without a sound body, it is possible for me to sin. May I never outlive my love for you or feel I no longer need your grace and tender mercy.

Through your Son, Jesus. Amen.

(Expanded from an anonymous source)